RISE OF THE NEW WORLD ORDER: BOOK SERIES UPDATES AND URGENT STATUS REPORTS-VOLUMES 1 THROUGH 5

J. Michael Thomas Hays

PREFACE

Back at the start of 2020 when the 'pandemic' was just starting, I was kicking myself because I had yet to assemble and publish Book 3 of my main "Rise of the New World Order" series.

It was going to be called "Rise of the New World Order 3: Resonance", and it was going to be mainly about geoengineering, which entails exploring and explaining how Tesla's 'HAARP' technology is being used against us.

After reviewing the facts coming out about the 'pandemic', it became very obvious to me that this was instead a 'planned pandemic', the plannedemic I call it. A false flag of epic proportions...their first global false flag to kick off the implementation of the prophesied global government.

My own 'terror alert' system went off the chart, and I knew I had to do something myself as a Sentinel to warn the people who looked to me for answers as to what was really going on. This was do or die, I had to sound the alarm by putting out these updates. I shifted focus from Book 3 to monitoring, researching and reporting on the current and ongoing situation.

As the plannedemic gained steam, the proponents of the New World Order moved quickly to set up a pseudo-police state to enforce quarantines, masking up the public, social distancing, tracking apps and generally terrorizing an unsuspecting public. So many things weren't adding up I started researching about it and became HIGLY concerned.

I knew in early 2020 that we were attacked by the evil ones with a bioweapon and the whole pandemic was staged in advance. I also knew that we would end up with mandatory vaccinations and vax passports, and we did.

Everything has come out about the plannedemic and has been reported on by yours truly the whole way, and I'm still covering it and putting out these updates as warranted. Update 6 was just released on 2/10/22.

A lot of people asked me to put these reports into paperback, so here they are, updates 1 through 5, unedited, exactly as they appeared to start with.

Thanks for your prayers and support, friends. -Sentinel Jeff Hays

TABLE OF CONTENTS

RISE OF THE NEW WORLD ORDER: BOOK SERIES UPDATE AND URGENT STATUS REPORT VOL. 1

MARCH 31, 2020

Well, friend…. this is not how I wanted for us to meet again. I thought we had more time but things are moving quickly now. As we descend into chaos I'm going to try and turn these 'reports' out as often as possible…as often as justified. Please look for me on Facebook, I've got two pages going now as I'm bounced in and out of Facebook jail because I'm trying to wake people up and keep them updated. These are largely NWO-themed meme and news pages but I post links for pertinent other stuff also.

Search for 'Samaritan Sentinel' and 'Rise of the New World Order: The Culling of Man's Meme Machine'. If I'm not actively posting there that means I'm in FB jail…or worse.

I just feel like I needed to say something about the current events to the people who read my books and woke up. This is the best way to reach a ton of people as hopefully Amazon will alert you to my update here. I put this out on Amazon's Kindle for as cheap as they would let me = 2.99. Hopefully Amazon will contact you about this update, you've got to prepare for the financial implosion that will be blamed on this 'pandemic', but it's really a 'plannedemic'.

I'll also try to put this out on my Facebook pages, but it's pretty long for a FB post. I'll definitely try though.

I certainly do appreciate people purchasing my books and spreading them around to support me and my family right now as always. Thank you in advance for your continued support!!!! There is no other book I know of that covers all the bases of the NWO like my first one.

The following should be taken under advisement **as my opinion only** and it is up to you to do your own due diligence in looking into and tracking everything I'm going to say.

I don't know for sure what's going to happen, but we just took a financial gut-shot from the alleged "pandemic" and effectively bankrupted the entire United States and even global travel industries of airlines, hotels, restaurants, etc.

These businesses might never come back. Why would they? To go broke next year over the next plannedemic? This is a gaping hole in our economy with millions now immediately on the unemployment ranks with not much future getting back into the same line of work because all those businesses are folding as you read this. You are witnessing the controlled demolition of our economy, and our country, the United States, right now, right before your eyes while we are all detained in 'soft' martial law for our own good against a virus that will kill less people than the flu. No, you don't want to catch this virus, I've heard nothing good about the illness, but what has been foisted upon the world is a false flag of epic proportions.

I will repeat this as I did for my first two books: Don't ever believe what I say without doing your own research and then coming to your own conclusions.

I am speaking on the authority of the amount of research I've done and continue to do, tips from others, and of course praying my heart out that I will know what to say when the time comes for people to look to me for guidance. I've woke up many thousands or more with my books and I'm not done yet speaking about what has happened and what I can see happening.

So...with all that said....

We've had the NWO/Illuminati/Deep Staters boxed in a corner now for a little while. All their pedophilia was uncontrollably spilling out in the public arena. Pizzagate, Jeffrey Epstein, Jimmy Seville, the Royal Family and tons more are horrible monsters to the point and degree it cannot be hidden any more.

All the names on Epstein's 'Lolita Express' flight manifests read like a who's-who of Hollywood elite, politicians, and European royalty. The cat was out of the bag and they were forced to act and act now or we would be coming for them with torches and pitchforks.

The globalist proponents of the Great Plan and their agenda for global enslavement were being threatened by a ton of people who are now awake thanks to you, me and others spilling the truth about the Federal Reserve, 9/11, Bilderberg, and the like.

We are on to them and they had to act and act fast as they were losing the information war and badly. I have literally spent tens of thousands of hours at this point researching and passing on information to others in my books and on Facebook...I live and breathe this stuff because that is what I was put here to do. When I woke up in 2007, I jumped right in the fight.

Unfortunately for us, they now use Artificial Intelligence to map out the NWO agenda these days, and apparently it called for releasing an engineered bioweapon against humanity to keep the Great Plan from being derailed.

They are probably going to pull it off with this plannedemic. There is the highest probability that this is the beginning of the End Game I'm afraid. It was always my intention to slow it down but it is moving full steam ahead.

You probably haven't heard this as this type of info is highly suppressed by the NWO-owned-and-controlled mainstream media, but the author of the U.S. Biowarfare Act has gone public stating he believes COVID-19 to be a BIOWEAPON that either escaped or was intentionally released. I believe the latter to be the truth. Watch this video interview on YouTube…as long as it is still up: https://youtu.be/F_TPjbu4FAE

They are not going to run us through this false flag and have millions more people wake up to the NWO, start looking for the truth about what is happening, start prepping, awakening others, etc. They are moving to quash the United States and humanity right now with this false flag called COVID-19.

We are in a bad way in terms of losing our country, and things are going to get way worse fast. This is a **'Red Alert'** status update, we've got a very rough road ahead of us. We've got an intentionally-released manmade bioweapon on one side and the empowered FEMA to "deal" with it, and the diabolical proponents of the New World Order who released the bioweapon on the other side and there is no where to run unless you have a rocket ship to Mars so buckle up.

Throw in an already-collapsed oil market, a soon-to-collapse stock market, and a dollar crisis not far behind and this is going to make for a truly interesting year. Oh yeah, we're supposed to hold an election or something also….almost the entire Federal Government is up for grabs this November.

Now it came out that some of the Congressmen and women sold their stock in hotels, etc. because they had beforehand knowledge of exactly what was going to happen. This whole thing is a gigantic false flag to protect the Deep State/Illuminati/New World Order crowd.

Why didn't they warn the hotels/restaurants/hair dressers/etc. that this financial storm was coming when they clearly knew it? Because they didn't want to cause panic. They are still doing this right now with Trump saying that he can't wait to get back to business in America. You can tell he is quite uncomfortable jerking us off like this because he too knows what's coming: FEMA martial law and the end of the USA.

So now we've got all the **MILLIONS** of hotel workers, restaurant workers, airlines people, etc. all unemployed and largely going on the government payroll via unemployment…they are now dependent on the state to survive going forward because those jobs aren't needed in the New World Order. That type of excess is coming to an end, slaves.

This is not good at all, we are headed straight into tyrannical fascism. The definition of fascism is when the state takes over all corporations. It also works the other way and this is why we are falling: the corporations have already taken over the government via lobbyists. Term limits and anti-lobbying laws could have prevented this but you know…everyone has their price. The entire federal government is bought and paid for by the Federal Reserve crowd!!!!!

I don't believe that we will pull out of the current financial nosedive we are in right now. This is probably going to be the big crash I talk about in my first book. This is why the Federal Reserve and Trump/Congress are all over this thing…throwing $2 Trillion dollars at it just to start with. Mortgage companies letting people slide for a year on their mortgages, SBA emergency loans available, etc. They know the shitstorm is right on the horizon. You can expect a roller coaster ride on Wall Street going forward…it will be one step forward, two steps back all the way down…possibly to ZERO.

I knew that the next crash after the 2008 one was going to be the big one, they just barely staved it off last time but this time it will be too big of an issue.

After what they did to stop the big crash in 2008 by using all their silver-bullets of interest rate reductions, this Greatest Depression is going to hit HARD.

They already ran the interest rates so low they can't really go lower without them paying you to borrow money…negative interest rates. Trump has publicly called for them himself!

The Fed right now is injecting money into the economy by buying "mortgage-backed securities". This is a fancy way of saying they are entering numbers on a computer screen to create hundreds of billions of dollars out of thin air and purchasing the rights to your house when they foreclose on it after this Greatest Depression gets rolling. Your house. Your neighbor's house. Your grandma's house. My house. All by printing money out of thin air for a small handful of globalist, satanic pedophiles.

Getting mad yet? I am….I am PISSED, pardon my French!!!

Some people were barely making it before this happened…I'm one of them! I'm not sure what I'm going to do but if enough people pass this report around, I'd move a few books and get some kind of plan together for my family's financial situation. I spent way too much time over the years working on waking people up instead of looking for work…my bad.

The lumber store down the street from my house is only open for 'takeout'….?????. Look I'm a construction worker. You just don't have a takeout/curbside lumber store…it just doesn't work like that. I'm a lifelong carpenter, I'm going to be hand-selecting the best lumber there is to make my work look as good as possible!!!

This isn't going to last long before everyone goes under like dominos and the whole thing crashes right to the ground….the whole pyramid scheme under the Federal Reserve is to thank for the coming financial woes.

Funny, that's why it was expressly stated in the Constitution to NOT EVER ALLOW AN ENTITY LIKE THE PRIVATELY-OWNED, FOR-PROFIT FEDERAL RESERVE TO EVER EXIST. And we let it in and gave the country's control to the evilest people on the planet: the Satanic pedophile murderous Illuminati banking families. You know exactly who they are from my first book!!!

You already know everything I'm talking about I hope…if you read my first book, I'm preaching to the choir here. It's just unfolding now before our eyes and it's like watching a horrific train wreck happen in slow motion, in real time.

And then when people are wondering what to do with the 'cash' they have in the bank after they barely sold their stock for pennies on the dollar.... their 'cash' being literally numbers on a computer screen and not gold in their pocket...you know...real money? They are going to implode the dollar either during or after the stock market meltdown and the dollar will then be worthless also.

The 2020 coronavirus plannedemic will be the scapegoat for the illegal, not-so-Federal Reserve's economy coming apart at the seams. This is an intentional, controlled demolition of our economy, just like the WTC on 9/11.

You know what's funny? The gooberment ran drills for this exact scenario last Fall!! The stock market will go to zero, then the dollar crisis will wipe out what is left. I wouldn't be surprised to see UN troops on the ground here before the end of the year. This is about a right time to get right with God if you haven't lately, because you might be going to see Him soon.

I fully am expecting riots to begin in the cities this year, either from people getting cabin fever or if the food starts to run out in the next few weeks/months, or whatever. People are broke right now, imagine not working at all for weeks or even months. This thing could drag on as long as they need it to in order to finish us off.

I also expect that we will be kicked when we're down. I'm fully anticipating a major earthquake in the United States and soon, I would say this year. With the HAARP technology available to the NWO they could easily trigger the Cascadia Subduction Zone earthquake right in my backyard in Seattle!!!

This would essentially destroy about every city up and down the West coast, coast of Japan, etc. This will be a HUGE quake with massive damage and massive loss of life. They were just running drills about it out here a couple years ago so that should tell you all you need to get your guard up!!

Now, going forward from today, Trump will eventually be blamed for the economic meltdown and the handling of the COVID-19 'plannedemic'. All voting this Fall will probably be electronic/mail-in and there will be no exit polls to police this election because I believe we may still be in quarantine later this year!

This elimination of exit polls will open the door to the proponents of the Great Plan to rig the election and install good ol' Hillary Clinton. Yes, I believe Hillary is going to be Biden's running mate, he will bow out or be removed, and Hillary will be in the driver's seat. Have you seen Hillary lately? She just got a bunch of plastic surgery in anticipation of her big day in the limelight as the "savior" of the U.S......*gag*. She would love to be the one to put the knife right the heart of the good ol' USA.

The Illuminati need their Jezebel in the driver's seat to put out the flames of all the pedophilia and general corruption we all know that they're up to.

Forced vaccinations are probably coming later this year and will be accompanied by attempted gun confiscation in the USA. I don't know if this will ignite a Civil War, but the death from the force-injected bioweapon they will label a 'vaccine' will arguably be worse than being shot with a gun so take your pick when the time comes. You will know what to do.

Going forward after this plannedemic blows over, 'Pandemic' will be the new invisible boogeyman to terrorize humanity. It was terrorism but that wasn't good enough. You can expect a mandatory annual 'pandemic' shot against whatever it is they cook up that year to go along with your flu shots, etc. No. Thank. You.

I doubt I'll be around that long anyways to be quite honest, I'm not very popular with what I've already done in the infowar against the NWO. I won't be taking any vaccine either. Nope.

They will introduce the new digital global currency, which of course they will issue and control....and legally mandate you use. The mainstream media is already quacking about the paper money and coin transmitting the virus. They want to go to a cashless society so they can track everything and it is unfolding right this second!!

The same people who set up the central bank pyramid scheme are the same ones who are setting up the global currency system. We're going digital people. RFID chipping of the population is right around the corner and actually has been practiced for many years at this point already. Soon it will be mandatory...arguably the Mark of the Beast.

I see Bitcoin being outlawed for the 'good of humanity' after the dust settles. Can't have any rogue currencies running around competing with the Satanists for control of the money supply and therefore humanity.

I also see gold confiscation coming, again, just like during the Great Depression. They want it all. Every last bit of it. For a dozen or so Satanic families pulling the strings of our reality.

Hey, it's Satan's world, says so right in the Bible. That's what my second book is all about, how we are in the clutches of Satan and his minions and always have been, that's how it was designed. They just do his bidding and have for thousands of years...and reap the rewards.

Now the game is coming to an end. Just as the Baby Boomers start checking out in large numbers, possible thanks to this coming plague called COVID-19, Gen X, the Millennials, Gen Z and beyond are all going to be left here to go through a literal Hell on Earth.

Even though we are staring down the oncoming crisis, it is still our duty to tell people what is really going on. To educate them with the truth of everything in my first book. What I learned by researching and writing my first book transformed me from an unbelieving atheist to a born-again Christian. The entire New World Order conspiracy is in the Bible if you have eyes to see and ears to hear the truth, this cannot be disputed if you've read my books.

I do believe I was always a saved man...I just didn't know it. Something had to trigger it and that something was knowing what was really going on in our world. There are still thousands and millions to wake up to this truth so they can claim their rightful place in the Book of Life. If they are saved, their names are in the Book of Life from the beginning of the world. I think that's somewhere in Revelation lol. They just need to be triggered...in a good way!

So many people have no idea what is happening that there almost needs to be a 'group awakening' or something. Unfortunately, only a very small percentage of people listen to what I'm saying and a HUGE percentage of people listen to useless talking heads on mainstream media...literally paid actors! None of them investigate ANYTHING or I wouldn't be writing these books!

I will tell you this, if I only were to wake up one person with my first book it would have been worth it, but I've woke up many more simply because I jumped in the batter's box and swung for the fence for humanity.

You yourself can get just as active and fast. Throw together a blog. Start doing videos. Start posting on message boards. These are what I was doing at the start before I had the motivation to go full throttle and write a book outlining all the pertinent stuff going on.

And that reminds me....the third book...*big sigh*

I'm so sorry it has taken this long....it's going to take a little while longer now. I was on track to get it done and out by the end of this year but I don't know what's going to happen now that we are heading into dire straits... hence this 'report'. This may be the last you hear from me! I'll sure try and get it done and out though.

I can let you know that the third book is way more like the first book in that I'm giving out a bunch of different topics and showing how they tie to the first book and the Great Plan for global enslavement.

The second book of the series, the Awakening, was more of a one-off but is super-pertinent information. I wish I would have had the second book as a separate, stand-alone book but what are you gonna do? That's what I get for doing everything myself right? Right. Author. Editor. Publisher. Advertiser. Promoter. I don't really know what I'm doing, I'm just making it up as I go!

Obviously, I'm getting help from above with all of this, because if you knew me personally, I'm a lifelong construction worker to the core. I'm pretty rough around the edges in other words. I'm still a beer-drinking, cussing, gun-totin' rock-and-rollin' patriotic guy and nobody, and I mean NOBODY needed to be woken up more than me back in 2007.

That spun my head right off when I woke up to the NWO and I went crashing to the ground as an unwashed atheist with no hope knowing about the NWO and that it was real.

Only a couple years into my research and Jesus spun my head back on straight, picked me up and dusted me off, and sent me off to write that first book.

And here we are now 7 years after releasing my first book and it's all coming true. I would be lying if I told you I wasn't a little scared, but I'm also a little excited. I really can't wait to shed this worn, physical body and get a one-way ticket outta Satan's world and into the loving arms of Jesus. We've all gotta die sometime, that's a fact, so no reason to be scared of it knowing your place is secure after the fact.

Never in our history...since the days of Nimrod's Babylon, has the world been so gripped by evil. Think about it. We have the most decadent society in the history of mankind. With the technology came great evil. Online porn. Tinder for random sexual hookups. Gay marriage. Trans kids...? WTH is that? We are in BIG TROUBLE.

So...I haven't worked on the third book for about three or four weeks now, just too much going on to get my head into it. But this mini-book you are reading now suddenly came together in just the last few days...I was suddenly moved to get something out there.

I just went and read the preface to the third book and got sick to my stomach as to how drastically things can change in life, and quickly.

Here is the preface for the third book as it was _INTENDED_ to be released later this year:

Well, I can hardly believe I've reached another milestone in my crazy life and managed to get my third book out but here we are. The world still hasn't ended and I'm still working my construction jobs and working on these books as I've got time available.

I've been doing a lot of 'memelording' since getting onto social media at the start of 2013 and I HIGHLY encourage you to join me and millions of others globally in this very effective campaign against the NWO. A picture says a thousand words. If you combine a powerful, thought-provoking picture or image, coupled with witty, biting, factual smarm, you have created a powerful propaganda tool and the NWO knows this.

*You would be amazed at how many people are awake around the world to the Great Plan. It doesn't matter if you are black, white, Latino, Asian, gay, straight, Christian, Hindu or whatever, the people running the planet want to cull the global population way down for easier control and **EVERYONE** is on the chopping block.*

There is an old saying, the enemy of my enemy is my friend. The enemy to humanity are the proponents of the New World Order, this makes all of humanity to be friends against the foe, the NWO. I don't care who you are, if you are awake and against the NWO agenda for global enslavement I've got your back, friend.

If you're already awake and have been doing research of your own, you may know some or all and even more than what I'm going to talk about here. Great. Awesome. Love it. Thank you from the bottom of my heart for taking a keen interest in our future. But if you are just waking up and recently coming off my last two books, you will find this a continuation in your crash-course about how the NWO operates.

In fact, part of the reason for this book 3 is if someone were to sit down and wake up for the first time, they would be able to read all three of my books straight through and have a better understanding of the NWO than 99.99% of the rest of the population. Another part of the reason for this book is hopefully I am bringing to even seasoned researchers some new information. And lastly, part of the reason for this book is to put into writing the facts of what is going on before they are censored from the internet by Google, Bing, YouTube, and the rest whose owners and controllers have been sucked into the Illuminati and now regularly attend Bilderberg meetings, Bohemian Grove campouts, attend CFR meetings and are on the Trilateral Commission, etc.

As with all of my books, as a whole they should be considered to be my opinion. Don't believe what I write as Gospel, research about what I write, but don't disbelieve out of hand as you read it either. I make my books as fact-based as possible to stand up to the naysayers.

Again, as with my first book, each chapter and subchapter in this book could have multiple books written about it and have been. I'm just bringing to your attention everything I think you should be made aware of at this point in time, just like my first book. I put everything in that book that I thought you needed to know to get at least a basic understanding of the New World Order. Now I have many new topics for you to look into and add to your arsenal of knowledge about what's really going on in our world.

People have no idea how good we have it today compared to 100 years ago in terms of creature comforts. At the same time, we also have it worse today because all of those things can be instantly taken away by our advanced technology.

For example, a single nuclear device detonated 250 miles above Kansas would cause an EMP that would knock out the national power grid and anything that needs electrical components to operate...which is about everything. This would instantly send us back to the 1800s. The cities' sewers would shut down and immediately begin to spill into the streets, rampant disease would immediately follow. Rape, robbery and murder would immediately commence upon those in the cities, especially if the guns are managed to be taken from the law-abiding.

This is a fact and there have even been Congressional hearings and public warnings generated about this so it's not a matter of if but when stuff like this is going to happen. They even tell you to have two weeks of survival supplies on hand. If you've read and followed my first book, you should actually have way more!

Look at how far we've fallen since the publication of my first book in January of 2013. Full-blown socialists occupying seats of our government at all levels. You should know by now that the New World Order is a socialist, anti-God/Jesus and pro-Satanic agenda run by the 'do as we say, not as we do' global elites.

*"**Bad men cannot make good citizens. It is impossible that a nation of infidels or idolaters should be a nation of freemen. It is when a people forget God that tyrants forge their chains. A vitiated state of morals, a corrupted public conscience, is incompatible with freedom**"*

-Patrick Henry, one of the Founding Fathers

The United States in particular is on the NWO's chopping block. A strong United States that the UN has no power over cannot be for much longer if things are to progress according to plan. We are the modern-day Babylon and we are slated to crash and burn...one way or another.

On June 26, 2015 the US Supreme Court legalized gay marriage nationwide. Gay marriage was just the beginning down the road to good ol' Sodom and Gomorrah. Now we've got 'trans kids' running around and we are expected to accept that that is the new societal norm. Now they are pushing for kids who aren't even old enough to decide their bedtime to decide if they want to undergo gender reassignment surgery...complete madness.

As an active member of the Truth Community I am pushing back against the lies and propaganda with everything I've got on social media as are others...and have paid the price being censored heavily, even banned for speaking my mind.

In particular, any opinion against the radical LGBT agenda is censored as 'hate speech'. If you are against pedophile drag queens hanging out in public libraries with unassuming parents with young, impressionable kids then you are a homophobe and not welcome on the liberal platforms of Facebook, Twitter, etc. We have fallen quite a way since I first woke up in 2007.

Since the publication of my last book in 2015 the banks and other major globalist corporations have installed RFID chips in all their debit/credit cards. These chips constantly track your location, buying habits, etc. and this information is collected and sold among the globalist entities. The next step from this is human implants, something that has already been happening for years now and is only increasing in usage.

Cancer rates are 100x what they were 100 years ago. As you know, we are under attack by land, sea and air.

Our GMO food is laced with biotoxins, pesticides and cancerous chemicals. It's not even food, it's a science experiment.

Fluoridated water is still the norm in the USSA, while being outlawed in about every other country on Earth.

The chemtrails/geoengineering are ramping up filling the air we breath with aluminum, barium, and who-knows-what-else.

We are exposed to millions of times more electromagnetic radiation than our grandparents were thanks to the proliferation of personal wireless devices: phones, tablets and laptops. The generally safe 'wired' desktop computer's numbers are declining as rapidly as the unsafe, radiation-spewing wireless devices are expanding. We're literally bathed in radiation these days and the closer you get to the city the worse it gets…another good reason to get out if you can.

The globalist drums are beating loudly for gun confiscation here in the United States thanks to a series of sloppy false flags that were picked apart by the Truthers.

Forced childhood vaccinations are now making their way through various local governments, again, largely pushed by government-worshipping statists.

__Keep in mind that I'm not a Republican, a member of the 'alt right' or any kind of ridiculousness like that.__ I am a Libertarian believing in less government and more freedom, something neither the left or right is behind. No matter who is the President, the globalist, one-world agenda marches forward.

Remember from my first book about the global warming hoax/scare? The United Nations propaganda machine has been rolling tough as of late to scare everyone into thinking that 'Climate Change' is going to doom us all if we don't turn over all aspects of human society to UN control. Just look where we're at with 'climate change' being shoved down our throats at every mainstream media propagandized moment. Greta Thunberg anyone?

This engineered storm of 'climate change' is purely to stampede humanity into the UN's waiting clutches. This physically involves using Tesla's various amazing technologies to affect the global weather and cause events that the UN is pinning on 'Climate Change'.

Just about all the hurricanes, fires and floods that are going on these days are not necessarily all caused by Tesla technology, but all can either be created, made worse or alleviated completely with said technology and I'm going to show you how in this book.

Not only can they affect the weather through 'geoengineering', they can affect us personally using Tesla's technology via radio frequency (rf) waves...including being able to literally insert voices in our heads! This is a fact that I will prove using the various patents on file stating they can do exactly this!

There are pressing things for you to be aware of and/or watch out for going forward. A lot of people are sensing the dangers around them but less are actually 'waking up' to the Great Plan for global enslavement.

If you are awake and know others that aren't you need to step up your game in sounding the alarm that things aren't right. I talk to people constantly about what's going on in the world I come into contact with when I'm out and about.

Pretty much everyone I personally know I've impressed upon them the information about the Federal Reserve being privately owned and controlling our economy and by default our country. Everyone is interested and concerned about money so this is always a good 'in' to get a conversation going about how the Fed, 9/11, the CFR, etc. are all connected through the ancient money powers headed by the Rothschild Banking Dynasty and buttressed by the Rockefellers and others to maintain a death grip over humanity.

So...This is arguably the true sequel to the first book....this is largely information I didn't know about at the time of the publication of my first book, and it took a few years of researching and just living as an awake soul to take it all in and see what else was out there that needed to be put into writing so the facts may live after information like this is struck from the internet like a hatchet against 'domestic terrorism'.

You mark my words because it's coming. Only the paper copies of my books will withstand the test of time. Files and notes on computers will easily one day be able to be remotely scrubbed of information. If you don't think the FBI, NSA, CIA and the rest aren't intimately involved with the development side of companies like Microsoft, Google, Amazon, etc. you haven't been paying attention.

People like Bill Gates and the founders of Google are all-in for the NWO, attending Bilderberg meetings, etc. Remember, money is power. Gates and Bezos have billions. The families who run the Great Plan are worth in the hundreds of trillions.

The people who run the Great Plan have been drawing interest on monopoly money for hundreds of years at this point. They constantly add to the amount of money in circulation (inflation) which they own to start with by printing out of thin air, then they loan it out to governments AT INTEREST remember. They are stacking coin left and right and we pay for it all!

"Compound interest is the eighth wonder of the world. He who understands it, earns it; he who doesn't, pays it."
-Albert Einstein

If you've made it this far and have read my first two books, I commend you for wanting to know as much as me. I want to know exactly, factually what is happening no matter how ugly the truth is.

I've never said that I know it all when it comes to the New World Order, but I want to. I want to know everything about what's happened with the Great Plan and what's going to happen.... most don't. Most can't handle knowing what we've learned so far and we're not done yet.

Now, my second book was and is extremely important information that I felt at the time was needed to lay the ground work for going forward. I'm not so sure now (lol). That book is vastly ahead of its time, even now, as there were no books on Saturn worship to be found on Amazon or the whole of the internet when I wrote that book and believe you me I looked because I am a voracious reader and wanted to know everything about ancient Saturn worship.

It is still largely the only book putting all the pieces together of ancient history and how Satan navigated his way through it collecting worship and adoration the whole way. Now that that's out of the way, off my plate, off my back, whatever you want to call it, we're back on track getting into the nuts and bolts operations of the Great Plan....the forward march to totalitarian world government and eventual (re)appearance of King Nimrod, aka the Antichrist.

A lot of people didn't like my last book, the Awakening, because they felt I gave too much attention to Satan. There is a **BIG** difference between attention and adoration. Hopefully they won't have a problem with me giving too much "attention" to Jesus and our Heavenly Father in this book 3, all entities need to be understood the best we can.

It's important to me personally since coming around and getting born-again during the research for my first book to try and figure out what He wants from us and why we're even here. I'm always asking myself questions and then trying to figure out the answer.

So what does He want? Adoration. It's actually very simple. Adoration is love, fear and respect all wrapped into one word. And what's Satan's #1 job right now in this world? To block that adoration by misleading us from all angles in order to transfer adoration to himself or his 'son' King Nimrod.

Look at what all the celebrities are doing flashing the occult signs, saying they are in the Illuminati, etc....it's because they really ARE Illuminati foot soldiers!!! Sure Jay-Z and the like are worth millions but their masters are worth TRILLIONS. All of this pedophile stuff coming out of Hollywood, Jeffrey Epstein, etc. is just the tip of the iceberg. The Satanic Great Plan is slowly but surely coming out into the open arena for all to see because we are ever near the End.

(End of Book 3 Preface)

So, friend, what do we do right now besides worry, fret, cower and let them run roughshod over us, our friends, family and way of life? You gotta get MAD and stand the up with me and millions of others and say NO!!! You CANNOT force-inject us. You CANNOT have our guns. You CANNOT force us to use an illegal digital currency issued by an illegal entity called the Federal Reserve! All of the preceding are illegal according to the Constitution.... HELP! HELP! HELP!!!!!

This whole pandemic is a false flag 'plannedemic'. Things you need to look into immediately about it include the following highly important issues:

-Event 201

-ID 2020

-CDC loses autism case

Quarantining the population will not stop this pandemic. When everyone comes out of their home detention there will be another wave of plannedemic. Only their vaccine will "stop it" so life can get back to normal... that's where the mandatory injections come in.

The CDC just lost badly in federal court and you probably never heard a peep about it. They lost a case to a non-profit who sued them over their statement that 'vaccines don't cause autism'. **The CDC could provide no proof of their statement so they lost in Federal court! This was completely whitewashed by the mainstream media.** Just another reason that this false flag is meant to take us down...we're on to them.

You've got time off now in 'quarantine'? **Get ACTIVE!!**

If nothing else help **ME** to get more active against the NWO! I've been trying to get on the Coast-to-Coast radio show for years and they won't even return my calls or email. Same with Alex Jones and others. I need **YOU** to email C2C, Alex Jones, and anyone else you can think of to get me on the air. My email is at the end of this report for a contact.

Nothing more I'd love than to be a monkey wrench in the gears of the NWO tyranny machine one last time but I need your help!!!! **I'M NOT AFRAID OF THEM** so saddle my horse, hand me my lance and watch me go right at them armed with faith and truth.

"But an hour is coming, and now is, when the true worshipers will worship the Father in spirit and *truth*; for such people the Father seeks to be His worshipers. God is spirit, and those who worship Him must worship in spirit and *truth*."
-John 4:23-24

Thanks for backing me up all these years and thanks for your support!!! Tell everyone you know about my first book and we'll see what happens. You never know, I pray that we can pull this current situation out of the fire but it's looking ominous, hence this report.

One last note before I sign off here, the artist for my book covers, and my friend, David Dees, has been diagnosed with stage IV cancer and is on the ropes. He's the original motivation for me to jump fearlessly into the fracas….thanks again David Dees, good luck on your recovery. He's forgoing traditional treatments like chemo and radiation and going the natural route. Please pray for him…we need him more than ever.

I pray for you daily my friends and allies, and hopefully you for me…I'm going to need it!!

Pray for the best but prepare for the worst.

RISE OF THE NEW WORLD ORDER: BOOK SERIES UPDATE AND URGENT STATUS REPORT VOL. 2

MAY 18, 2020

Table of Contents

Intro

"Nearly every American citizen is suspect under the Patriot Act. Cameras are everywhere if you take the time to look around and notice them, tracking everything you do. Just look up at the traffic signals the next time you are in any decent-sized town. A good deal if not all of these cameras are equipped with facial-recognition and license plate-reading software.

These are not only monitoring but recording everything that comes into the lens and stored, just in case they need it. It costs next to nothing to store information these days, and they are storing as much information as possible.

We are constantly pushed to stop using cash or checks and to go with "automatic debit" to pay our bills, and on the other end "automatic credit" for our paychecks, whereby we don't even hold in our hand the money we earned from working an honest day's labor—it's just numbers on a computer screen, all tracked by "big brother".

Virtually your entire life has been recorded and is on computer records somewhere, and if you are suspected to be a combatant against the New World Order agenda, these records will be assembled together in some Homeland Security office, and your case will be assigned to one of the HS lackeys to "keep an eye on you".

This means this person will be constantly reviewing everything you do, everything you buy, what websites you go to, where you drive your car and what places you visit, looking for anything to build a case against you as a domestic terrorist.

If they feel they have enough "evidence" that you are a threat to the Great Plan agenda, and if you haven't fallen into one of their pitfalls, they will just flat out arrest you with no reason needed or given, and send you to a FEMA camp, or worse to Guantanamo, probably never to be heard from again and all "legal" under the NDAA signed by Fuhrer Obama at the end of 2011.

We are also headed for a national ID card system complete with RFID location-tracking chips. Once that is implemented and accepted by the sheeple, *they will take it to the next level: Personal RFID microchipping, either by implantable chip or RFID tattoo, with both of these options in existence right now.*

RFID stands for Radio Frequency Identification, and allows you to be tracked by GPS anywhere on the planet. I'm not talking about injecting a small chip under your skin either, they can in fact do it now with an RFID tattoo, and if you don't believe this you better Google it, because that is a fact. Be vigilant for false flag events concerning information security that could make RFID chipping mandatory by law.

There are about 900 drone (unmanned) airplanes flying over the U.S. at the beginning of 2013, and that number is projected to skyrocket to 30,000 within 10 years. Why so many drones over the U.S.? It's part of the Homeland Security police state they are implementing. And they are all already equipped with facial recognition software and……maybe assassination implements for the most patriotic dissenters in the future? That's what they are doing right now in Afghanistan: assassinating the "troublemakers", and any men, women, and children who happen to be in the immediate vicinity.

Look for this to start happening in the U.S. at some point in the future, literally "Death from above".

The way they are going to excuse quickly bringing in this tyrannical behavior is through declaring martial law in the United States.

There are a handful of scenarios laid out in the FEMA guidelines that allows the federal government to declare martial law and suspend the Constitution. This will be accomplished with one of many different false flag scenarios that we already know are in the works due to vigilant people researching these kinds of things.

Remember what a false flag is: an orchestrated event to get the people to capitulate to what the Great Plan needs to advance, but otherwise wouldn't go along with it. An orchestrated event like the coming economic collapse most likely, but time will in fact tell.

It was actually made public in the Mainstream Media recently that Homeland Security had purchased 2 billion rounds of 9-millimeter and .40 caliber hollow-point bullets specifically to arm their employees with and also to distribute to other federal agencies across the country.

Hollow-point bullets are made to do one thing: inflict maximum tissue damage to a human in the hopes of a single shot being a kill shot. Now why would they be doing this? Is something going to happen that the feds know about that hasn't been put out in the Mainstream Media to alert the public? They wouldn't keep us in the dark, would they? You already know the answer to that question.

2 billion bullets are enough to pump 6 rounds into every man, woman, and child in America. What are they planning on doing with all of this ammo except to use it and soon.

Let's go over some of the potential scenarios that I feel are possible, or _probable_, so that when the next false flag event happens, you will know the _truth_ of what is really going on.

We already went over the economic crash that's coming, the likes of which has never been seen before. The dollar is currently the reserve currency of the world and won't be in the near future. This spells disaster for the citizens and country of the United States of America.

As the derivatives pyramid comes crashing down, the Federal Reserve will begin to "print" money en masse to try and contain the fire. This will not work, hyperinflation will ensue, and the dollar will crash. This means that the dollar will become worthless, and if you have your wealth in the form of United States dollars, you will be financially ruined.

The economic conditions that gave rise to Hitler are coming again x 100. The reason for the crash will be blamed on the Federal Reserve and the other central banks. The Federal Reserve and the rest of the individual nations' central banks will implode or be abolished. This will pave the way for the introduction of the ultimate one world central bank, of course owned by the Illuminati families.

Again, when this massive economic crash happens, you will know that is was coming, who did it, how it happened, and why they did it.

As the worldwide central-bank pyramid scheme falls like a house of cards, bringing worldwide economic and societal collapse, expect pestilence and disease to go off the chart as the power grids break down, sewers quit operating, drinkable water quits flowing into the cities and countries, and generally unsanitary conditions explode.

This would probably be a good time for the operators of the Great Plan to introduce a worldwide flu pandemic.....or worse.

Another way, all by itself, to introduce martial law is through a massive pandemic. Military scientists exist whose sole job purpose is to create deadly bioweaponry for the New Babylon's military use.

This is where that anthrax came from immediately after the attacks on 9/11. If you research what our military is in possession of in terms of weaponized biological agents intended to be used against human beings, it is truly frightening.

A massive outbreak of an engineered, highly contagious, highly deadly virus would not only excuse martial law to "limit the spread of the disease", it would eliminate millions, if not ultimately billions of humans from the planet.

Remember, the elimination of 90% of the Earth's population is one of the goals of the Great Plan.... the Culling of Man.

Don't worry though, I'm sure the Illuminati and their families will have the needed vaccines to be able to live and carry on for us all.

The military, under the direction of the proponents of the Great Plan who run the government, have built massive underground cities for the elites to go and hide out in just in case something like a massively deadly and contagious pandemic breaks out...

-From my first book, "Rise of the New World Order 1: The Culling of Man", released January of 2013, **Chapter 12/B: What's Going to Happen**

Well…hello again my friend…long time no talk!

I've decided that we're going to go down with the ship together, I plan on releasing these reports every few weeks now as our situation continues to deteriorate. I'm researching as we go, filtering and fact-checking everything as best as possible. Censorship on Google of pertinent information is getting worse by the day at this point. I'm glad I've got my first two books done and out, a permanent record of the truth.

Obviously and as always, what I present in my books should be taken as my educated opinion and not as gospel. All of my books are my *opinion*, based on *facts*. Due diligence is up to you to research everything I talk about and come to your own conclusions. I'm just telling you what I believe and why.

I was always taught growing up if someone was doing you wrong you speak up and call that right out to the point of physical altercation if it comes down to it to stand up for yourself.

I am vastly too disgusted, bewildered and angry to sit on my hands while Bill Gates walks around like a humanitarian in the public eye when he's anything but…truly an agent of the global pedo-Satanists.

This psychotic Bill "Baal" Gates started our country on fire and then shows up in a fire truck…with hoses full of poisonous vaccines.

Time is too short to keep my powder dry…our country in the jaws of the NWO Beast as I speak. Please print up this report if you're able and pass out!!!

Print these reports up on hard paper to share with others as things go right to hell. If you are able, get the paperback of my first book, you can read it aloud to family and neighbors after all electronic traces of the Truth Movement are eliminated…which includes all digital forms of my book. We are right there, folks.

People have to know what Gates & co. are up to and it's all in this second report.

Hmmm...well the official narrative as of the publishing of this update is that COVID-19 came from a bat in the Chinese wet market in Wuhan.

In the days leading up to the publishing of this report there is scuttlebutt coming out of the White House that mounting evidence suggests that COVID-19 came out of the biological lab in Wuhan, China.

Fauci is still insisting it came from a bat, while the evidence is mounting that it is what I and a ton of others have been saying, it's an engineered bioweapon.

If it can be PROVEN UNEQUIVOCALLY that it was made in a lab their little plan of releasing a 'mutated' version of it here in the next couple of months might be too risky and they would be called out by the independent medical community more so like they are right now...humanity is on to them.

The heat is starting to come upon Bill Gates, Dr. Fauci and others...as well as Trump. This is going to get very interesting, not that it hasn't been a shitshow up to this point....geez what a nightmare, particularly for the vulnerable citizens of our country, the old, young, handicapped...this is terrible...I want some payback and right now dammit. Pass me my torch and pitchfork, please.

Whether it came out of that Wuhan lab or not, I do believe that it is real and is a bioweapon that was intentionally released in Wuhan, knowing it could be used to cripple the global economy and the United States in particular. It is a weapon of the NWO against humanity to destroy life as we know it and usher in the New World Order. It is not even as dangerous as the flu from what I can ascertain, at least for now.

We are almost out of time to slow or stop them. This update report contains a blistering accounting of Bill Gates' cumulative actions and his henchman Fauci, and will now be a chapter in the upcoming Rise of the New World Order 3: Harmageddon.

Another HIGHLY CREDIBLE person has come forth since the publication of my last book also stating that this is a man-made virus and didn't come out of a 'wet market in Wuhan'. This man's testimony has been completely whitewashed by the mainstream media. There are plenty of people calling BS on the "naturally occurring bat-origin of COVID-19" at this point.

There was talk in the online Truth community in March of COVID-19 being a 3-part bioagent: one-part HIV, one-part malaria, and one-part coronavirus.

The one-part malaria would explain why the drug hydroxychloroquine works so well because it's an anti-malaria drug! Trump was lambasted for promoting this early on but it really does work effectively against COVID-19…imagine that.

Now check **THIS** out…

Luc Montagnier, the French virologist and **Nobel Prize winner** for his work on HIV, said the SARS-CoV-2 virus (COVID-19) was created in a laboratory by inserting genes from HIV, the AIDS virus, into a coronavirus!!!

"We have concluded that this virus was created," said the French scientist, during an interview with the French channel CNews.

In 2008 Montagnier won the Nobel Prize in Medicine for his part in research that led to the discovery of HIV, so this guy isn't some dummy!

"There has been a manipulation of the virus: at least part of it, not all of it. There is one model, which is the classic virus, which comes mainly from bats, but to which HIV sequences have been added, in any case, it's not natural. It's the work of professionals, of molecular biologists. Very meticulous work. For what purpose? I don't know. One hypothesis is that they wanted to create an AIDS vaccine"

Montagnier went on to cite a study by a group of researchers at the Indian Institute of Technology in New Delhi, which found "an uncanny resemblance" and "little chance of coincidence" in the amino acid sequences of a SARS-CoV-2 and HIV-1 protein.

Montagnier also predicted COVID-19 should be going away soon, its artificial origin would be weakening it.

"One can do anything with nature, but if you make an artificial construction, it is unlikely to survive. Nature loves harmonious things; what is alien, like a virus coming from another virus, for example, is not well tolerated. So what we're seeing is that in the western United States, in Seattle, the sequences are destroyed, virtually non-existent. So, if the pathogenic power of the coronavirus is linked to the insertion of these sequences, we can think that it's going to disappear."

I agree. It's going to disappear. Then it's going to come back, 'mutated', and will be more contagious and dangerous. Gates, Fauci, the WHO, the corrupt CDC and all the rest of the 'experts' have all stated another wave of pandemic is coming.

Again, Fauci has gone pubic in the last few days to state that COVID-19 is a NATURALLY OCCURRING VIRUS and at this point we all know that is just a flat out LIE and he knows it!!

Most people are buying into thinking Gates is an 'expert' on viruses and vaccines purely because he is rich and famous. They aren't even batting an eye about his agenda because 'he's the richest man in the world'.

Ummm….if you look into it he didn't get rich by being a nice guy but by being a completely diabolical JERK!

This is the same Bill Gates who has said on one hand that **we need to cull back the global population using vaccines**, and on the other is **claiming to be the savior of humanity with his vaccine** that will keep the population from being decimated by COVID-19…..he's a lying snake. He's a true Rothschild/Rockefeller puppet. You've seen him smiling smugly on the teevee with his sweater, trying to appear to be meek and harmless.

Nothing could be further from the truth!!! Gates is a cutthroat corporate kingpin who got to the top by stealing ideas and ruthlessly eviscerating his competition until Microsoft stood alone at the top of the personal computer world. His ideals come from his father, a hardcore eugenicist!!!

He's also a do-as-I-say-not-as-I-do elitist, which ALL of the upper echelon of the NWO are.

Besides corporate piracy and vaccines, Gates is also a 'climate change' activist. That's funny, he just bought a multi-million-dollar mansion on the coast somewhere a few weeks ago...won't it be flooded when all the glaciers melt from climate change? These people are saying one thing and doing another!

Sure, Gates is way up the financial ladder but remember, Gates' billions **PALE IN COMPARISON TO THE TRILLIONS CONTROLLED BY THE PROPONENTS OF THE NEW WORLD ORDER**.

Gates is a PIKER. A PUPPET. Why do you think he was caught photographed with Jeffrey Epstein? To compromise him to the NWO puppet masters.

You've never seen a Rothschild or Rockefeller with Epstein or in any of his 'Lolita Express' jet airplane flight manifests, right? Right. But they got Gates' hands dirty with Epstein and arguably even before that.

In fact, Gates seems to have been helped along his entire career to get to this point...No, that's the stuff of conspiracy theories....*rolls eyes*

If you really dig into how Microsoft came into being, you'll see exactly what I'm talking about. At the least, they have pedo-dirt on Gates and if he doesn't do exactly as they say they will ruin him in the public eye....or worse. He knows their power, as do we.

The Satanic Rothschild/Rockefeller/Royal Family are the pinnacle of the global Satanic network. Notice how Prince Andrew got tangled up with Epstein and walked away a free man even with victim eyewitness testimony against him IN PUBLIC...he was never meant to be compromised like Gates or others as he was born into the BIG CLUB.

Now, puppet-boy Gates has 'his' vaccine that is coming....hooo boy. ☹

This vaccine was created years ago when they were planning this whole thing out and is intended to either maim or kill you outright eventually and bring you under full NWO-dependence...we'll have to wait and see.

No matter what happens with the vaccine, remember, whoever supplies it won't be held accountable thanks to the **1986 Vaccine Injury Act!!!!** You've got to wake others up to this **FACT!!!!**

Either way, I'm not taking it, or my family, or any of my friends, or ANYONE I've talked to about this....everyone is waking up, and that's why they will hit us hard in the 'second wave'. It will be contagious and far more deadly. They need it to be in order to stampede the sheeple into wanting the vaccine that is coming.

Gates' Instagram, Facebook and other pages are now under constant crushing attack by the Truth Movement...YAY!!!!!!!!!!!!!!!!!!!!!!!!!!

I've been party to this myself, opening up an Instagram account purely to get at Gates and others and I HIGHLY ENCOURAGE you to do so also.

Here is a sampling of what was posted on Gates' Instagram before he pulled this particular post:

"Go to HELL. We're on to your secret societies"

"Are you even human? How could you be OK with what you're doing to the world?"

"Quit pushing your garbage vaccine. We don't want it"

"Operation 'Bill Gates Wants To Depopulate The Planet' is underway. First comes the plandemic, next comes the microchip vaccine that will kill more than the virus. WE DO NOT CONSENT TO YOUR POISON!!!! #billgatesisevil

"SAY NO TO VACCINE"

"#killbill2020"

"I love that he (Gates) is being dragged. So many awake"

"If you think Gates is a Satanist, give me a like" (This was the number one comment in terms of upvoting...!!!)

Exercise your Constitutional rights while you can because they will soon be gone if you don't...ALL HANDS ON DECK SENTINELS!!!

The powers-that-be, aka the CDC/FDA/NIH crime bosses, have publicly stated to little fanfare that they are allowing this 'new' vaccine to be rushed through without even animal testing because this is *'such an emergency...the economy and society won't recover unless we eradicate COVID-19 like smallpox'* or whatever BS-excuse they will spit out.

'*Rushing it through'* for the '*good of humanity'* will be the excuse for not discovering the 'side effect' of extreme injury and/or DEATH that will start to show up months or YEARS after this injection. The culling of man is at hand!!! This is not a drill.

Again, the **Vaccine Injury Act of 1986** is still in place so no matter what happens with the rushed vaccine the manufacturer won't be held liable... especially Baal Gates!!!!

You want to talk about a Zombie Apocalypse....everyone that gets the vaccine....OMG....good night. Stop the world, I want off...this is complete madness. A literal nightmare scenario is coming right up folks.

With that said, I'm going to release my long-overdue Book 3, "Harmageddon", in pieces through Amazon's Kindle program.

I'm not a big fan of globalist Bezos, but they are the only game in town for a self-published, go-it-alone author-activist to reach people like I have and do. No big publisher would dare touch what I've got to say about the facts of our situation!! I'll eventually have all the parts together later this year to put them together in a true book 3 that I can submit for paperback production. In the meantime, KDP/Amazon are what I'm working with.

I certainly do appreciate your financial support, when you purchase my books it helps me to be able to keep researching, writing and releasing my books and update reports like this one. I also SUPER-APPRECIATE reviews you leave on Amazon...those really do help me out also...if you WANT to help, I'll sure accept it. I need everything you can back me up with now or never...Thank you!!!!!!!!!!!!!!

If you've read my first update through Amazon, I've set this up as a series so I'm hoping they will just straight up notify anyone who's read part 1 that part 2 just went live.

Of course, we might not even talk after this report! If not, thanks for joining me on this wild ride of finding out what's really going on, truly terrifying but spiritually enlightening to the max!

I'm glad I know the **FACTS** I do; I hate wondering about stuff...drives me crazy. Tell me the ugly truth over a beautiful lie any day. At least I can make hugely important, life-altering decisions that way based on facts instead of deceptions and lies.

This particular report is obviously my take on current events as I write and edit this report, but I've decided it's highly important for both you and me to know about "Slow Kill Bill" Gates. He's been on my radar for a while now, he's had quite a reputation as chief of Microsoft.

In fact, let's figure Bill out right now and then we'll get to the rest of the update.

I've decided there will be a chapter on Gates in Book 3, what you will read in this report. It will be worded slightly different and maybe more info, but this is basically what you need to know about eugenicist Bill and his urgent agenda to vaccinate and track the entire global population...anything for his masters.

'Slow Kill Bill' Gates

The recent public narrative about Gates has not been the old 'usual' of the ruthless head of the Evil Empire itself, Microsoft.

Now he's depicted in the media as a mild-mannered, caring, concerned, sweater-wearing, constantly-smiling billionaire philanthropist throwing billions of dollars of his own money around to make the world a safer place.

Gates pursues his ambitions by bankrolling the World Health Organization---an arm of the UN---and the CDC---an arm of Big Pharma---and by working with these organizations and others he donates billions to in order to facilitate vaccine development and technology in general that will help bring the third worlders up out of poverty.

What a load of BS!!!

Gates and co. have no intention of bringing the third world standard of living up to the first world standard. They are seeking to do the opposite actually. The citizens of the USA, Europe and other 'advanced' nations are soon to know what it feels like to starve to death. The proponents of the NWO are going to flip the script!

"**First, we've got population. The world today has 6.8 billion people. That's headed up to about nine billion. Now, if we do a really great job on new vaccines, health care, reproductive health services, we could lower that by, perhaps, 10 or 15 percent ...**"

-Bill Gates, 2010 'TED talk'

When Gates says "reproductive health services" he means that his people are actively sterilizing and euthanizing Africans and Asians via vaccines, birth control and abortions!

Bill Gates' ideals, motivations and moral compass come from his father, eugenicist Bill Gates Sr.

Here is a portion of a transcript of an interview between Bill Moyers and Bill Gates in 2003:

GATES: *Certainly, I'll never be able to put myself in the situation that people growing up in the less developed countries are in. I've gotten a bit of a sense of it by being out there and meeting people and talking with them. And one of the gentlemen I met with AIDS talked about how he'd been kicked out of where he'd lived and how he felt awful he'd given it to his wife and their struggle to make sure their child didn't have it, and the whole stigma thing, which, you know, that's hard to appreciate. In this country when you get sick people generally reach out, you know, that's the time to help other people and yet some of these diseases it's quite the opposite.*

So, what I was thinking about was where my resources that I'm the steward of be able to make an impact, I thought "okay, what's the greatest inequity left?" And to me, and the more I learned about health and the unbelievable inequity, it kind of stunned me, it shocked me, every step of the way.

MOYERS: *You could have chosen any field, any subject, any issue and poured billions into it and been celebrated. How did you come to this one? To global health?*

GATES: *The two areas that are changing in this amazing way are information technology and medical technology. Those are the things that the world will be very different 20 years from now than it is today.*

I'm so excited about those advances. And they actually feed off of each other. The medical world uses the information tools to do their work. And so when you have those advances you think will they be available to everyone. Will they not just be for the rich world or even just the rich people and the rich world? Will they be for the world at large?

The one issue that really grabbed me as urgent were issues related to population... reproductive health.

And maybe the most interesting thing I learned is this thing that's still surprising when I tell other people which is that, as you improve health in a society, population growth goes down.

You know I thought it was...before I learned about it, I thought it was paradoxical. Well if you improve health, aren't you just dooming people to deal with such a lack of resources where they won't be educated or they won't have enough food? You know, sort of a Malthusian view of what would take place.

And the fact that health leads parents to decide, "okay, we don't need to have as many children because the chance of having the less children being able to survive to be adults and take care of us, means we don't have to have 7 or 8 children." Now that was amazing.

MOYERS: *But did you come to reproductive issues as an intellectual, philosophical pursuit? Or was there something that happened? Did come up on... was there a revelation?*

GATES: *When I was growing up, my parents were always involved in various volunteer things. My dad was head of Planned Parenthood. And it was very controversial to be involved with that. And so it's fascinating. At the dinner table my parents are very good at sharing the things that they were doing. And almost treating us like adults, talking about that.*

Yes, what Gates said in this interview is apparently true, otherwise why would he have said it, but I cannot find anything about it online: Bill Gates Sr. was head of the national abortion mill called Planned Parenthood.

It only says online that he was on the board of Planned Parenthood at some point, but I believe Billy Junior was telling the truth in the interview.

Now that sonny-boy 'Slow Kill Bill' has moved to the top of the global financial food chain, Bill Sr.'s ambitions have now been empowered. The Bill and Melinda Gates Foundation is at the pinnacle of the globalist eugenicist ambitions of the NWO masters. Gates Sr. sits on the board of the Bill and Melinda Gates Foundation and is a co-chair and ultimately, it's director, since all this eugenics crap was his baby to start with. Bill jr. is just picking up the torch for his father.

It should be noted that Bill Sr., Bill Jr. And Melinda are all card-carrying Democrats, all pro-abortion, pro-open borders, pro-globalist, etc. In the 2016

Wikileaks dump it was even revealed that Hillary Clinton had considered Bill Gates as her VP pick!! They would not have even considered that if Gates was a conservative by them. Not that I'm a conservative myself...you know me by now.

The governor of Washington State where I live, Jay Inslee-his daughter works for the Bill and Melinda Gates foundation, so everything is nice and cozy in Washington and Seattle for Gates and co.

Melinda Gates, speaking at the 2019 G7, pushed for digital currency in order to help empower women. Melinda is a known Bilderberg attendee, as is Bill. They are complete NWO-operatives.

Gates was busted associating with notorious pedophile Jeffrey Epstein. Gates' name is in at least one flight manifest on the 'Lolita Express' to Epstein's Pedo-Island in the Caribbean.

Gates knew what he was doing. He vehemently denies ever being on that flight!!! But he was!!!

It is written in stone on the Georgia Guidestones to maintain humanity at 'not more than 500 million' and it looks like they are going to make a run at that with the upcoming economic devastation, food shortages, dangerous vaccines and general chaos that the proponents of the New World Order have managed to kick off with little to no resistance from society.

Gates seems to be in the driver's seat of all of this chaos, telling people to quarantine and that there will be no 'normal' until the entire world is vaccinated. Who the hell put him in charge? He's a private citizen and not an elected-anything so sit down little boy Bill, we don't need your 'help'.

How did this punk Bill Gates get the money and power needed to realize his father's ambitions? He schemed, bullied and pirated his way to the top ala John D. Rockefeller.

Bill Gates Jr. was positioned with $50,000 from somewhere, probably his daddy, to purchase the program that would become MS-DOS...Gates didn't invent anything!! He then somehow got his foot in the door to license this product to IBM in a hugely shady deal if you look into it.

It was revealed in his co-founder Paul Allen's memoir, "Idea Man", that Allen stated Gates was a ruthless schemer who demeaned his employees and conspired to rip him off personally of his percentage of Microsoft ownership!!

He stated that Gates was after every bit of the company he could get when it came time to issue stock and Allen felt bullied, getting less of a share than he felt he deserved. Allen also stated he overheard Gates and Steve Ballmer conspiring against him to lessen his stake in the company even more!! Gates is truly a jerk that thinks little of humanity like he does his employees! This is documented in co-founder Allen's book!

Gates brutish approach to business and competition that led Microsoft to the top peaked in February of 2000 when he was forced to step down as CEO of Microsoft as part of a deal with US government prosecutors over anti-trust legislation against Microsoft. There is much more to this story, but you get the gist.

Gates bowed out of Microsoft with billions upon billions of dollars' worth of stock.

What's the first thing he did when he 'left' Microsoft? He started his own tax-free foundation of course to squirrel away those billions from the tax man…sound familiar? Then made a big deal about it in public like he was some kind of hero!! What is there NOT to hate about this guy? We're just getting started!

Not wanting to keep all his eggs in one basket, or his fingers in one piece of the NWO-pie as it were, Gates started getting involved in all manners of NWO-related mechanisms.

Let's start with the organized dumbing down of America called 'Common Core'…yes, Gates is primarily responsible for Common Core!!! A dumbed-down America would be much easier to collapse and make dependent on a world government to save them from themselves.

Starting with $200 million in 2008, Gates bankrolled the program and also the political strings that needed to be pulled in order to institute Common Core nationwide…which they did.

Once Obama got sworn in at the start of 2009, the then-President Obama swiftly worked to implement Gates' Common Core nationwide. Just a couple of good ol' modern day progressive Democrats looking out for the USA…ugh.

10+ years, $400+ million of Gates Foundation money, and hundreds of billions of taxpayer-education funds after the implementation of Common Core, and we're no more ahead than when we started and are arguably behind. In 2017, Gates finally admitted Common Core was a failure.

Wow. See how much *evil* influence this guy has already had over us and our nation? He never intended to make our kids smarter at all, quite the opposite!!! He is a full-on NWO-puppet boy.

After Gates started his foundation and had access to tax-free money, he started to diversify his holdings….

In 2010 he threw out some pocket change to the tune of $23 million and bought 500,000 shares of ~~Monsatan~~ Monsanto.

He stated the following on GMOs in a 2016 Wall Street Journal interview:

"What are called GMOs are done by changing the genes of the plant, and it's done in a way where there's a very thorough safety procedure, and it's pretty incredible because it reduces the amount of pesticide you need, raises productivity (and) can help with malnutrition by getting vitamin fortification. And so I think, for Africa, this is going to make a huge difference, particularly as they face _climate change_ …"

The fact is, Bill, that most GMO crops are intended to be ~~sprayed~~ bathed in toxic Roundup, which contains cancer-causing Glyphosate, the active ingredient in Monsanto's 'Roundup' weed killer.

The plants are genetically altered to be able to withstand the Roundup, but the weed killer kills everything else around it, including the people, and then goes on to contaminate the soil, water, air and everything else.

I've looked extensively into Roundup and glyphosate is just toxic, let alone the other even WORSE chemicals that are put in it that are labeled 'inert ingredients' making them immune from listing on the label!!!

Gates stated that there is a 'very thorough safety procedure' involved in making and testing GMOs.....GIVE ME A BREAK! These GMOs are DESIGNED from the get-go to be bathed in toxic poison!!

I saw that Gates had recently partnered with global AG magnate Cargill to start introducing GMO soy into Africa. So the people there are already starving, let's give them Frankenfood that that have to bathe in toxic chemicals to make it work and poison their land and people. Perfect. Thanks Slow Kill!!

The recently retired head of the Gates Foundation's agricultural research and development team was Rob Horsch, a former decades-long Monsanto employee. Vultures of a feather, flock together.

In 2016 Bayer bought Monsanto, kept their products/name brands, and dropped the Monsanto name. The toxic products are still there, just under the wholesome **Bayer** banner.

This is the same Bayer that, among other things, **kept HIV-infected medicines on the market in third world countries after pulling them in the USA after it was discovered they were contaminated with HIV**.... they literally murdered thousands of people intentionally with their tainted medicine for hemophiliacs, most of them children.

Moving on to the next NWO-themed action Gates has inserted himself in....

At the end of 2018, it was publicly announced that Bill Gates would be teaming up with Harvard scientists...meaning he was bankrolling them and they would be answering to him...to do experiments in injecting solid particles into the atmosphere to block the Sun in the hopes of mitigating 'climate change' or 'global warming' or whatever they are calling their climate charade now. Hey Gates! You might want to talk to the military, they have been spraying us like bugs for YEARS and are PROS at blocking out the Sun on any given day.

And go figure: As I was putting this report together, it was announced that Gates was teaming up with Tyson Foods and others to start making artificial meat. This meat would take cultured meat cells and regrow the meat in laboratories. Mmmmmm......tasty labmeat....soylent green can't be far behind at this point.

So...on to the Big Kahuna that Gates has taken upon himself: Vaccines

I'm going to do a status update report on vaccines specifically coming right up, certainly will be a chapter in Book 3, so let's just talk about Gates' relation to vaccines in general now instead of the mechanics behind the actual vaccine components.

To start with, the Gates Foundation donations to the WHO are second only to the United States contributions. This is the group who gets to decide---by whose authority I don't know---when a disease 'officially' turns into a global 'pandemic'. They are also the front that Gates uses to inject (!) his influence into third world countries and ultimately the entire planet.

The WHO was founded in the 1940s along with about the rest of the globalist, pro-NWO organizations. WHO = 1948. UN = 1945. World Bank = 1944. Etc....ad nauseum.

The WHO is basically an arm of the United Nations, and from my first book you know who founded and runs the UN even to today: the proponents of the New World Order. Remember, the UN was built right on land donated by the Rockefellers!!

Virtually everyone to do with this plannedemic and the upcoming COVID-19 vaccine are on Gates Foundation payroll: The WHO, CDC, National Institute of Health/NIH, Dr. Fauci, Dr. Birx, all of it....all are in the pocket of Bill Gates and his Deep State masters.

Gates plays dirty pool and has all his life. Now he's got his own puppet, Dr. Fauci, who he's using as a battering ram against the USA to get us all to quarantine and destroy our own economy, our rights, our morale, our country. This whole quarantine has been an uncalled-for DISASTER for our country.

You better brush up on Fauci too. He is going to be front and center in your life for the next few months or years. He is almost as important to know about as Gates, so let's do this!

Anthony Fauci was born in Brooklyn in 1940, the son of a pharmacist. He was raised in a strict Roman Catholic household, first Communion at 7 and confirmed at 12 years of age.

He was schooled by Jesuits at Regis High School in New York City, and went to College of the Holy Cross, Founded in 1843 by the Society of Jesus (Jesuits) in Worcester, Massachusetts.

Now, you know all about my position on the Unholy Roman Empire and its NWO foot soldiers the Jesuits.... 'nuff said. Fauci should be regarded as a Jesuit agent on your scorecard, right next to Lady ~~CaCa~~ GaGa.

Well the love of Jesus Christ allegedly wasn't spiritually fulfilling enough for Fauci after he left school and ultimately came to be what is called a 'humanist'...by his own admission.

<u>"Broadly and generically, I'm not a regular church attender. I have evolved into less a Roman Catholic religion person [to] someone who tries to keep a degree of spirituality about them. I look upon myself as a humanist. I have faith in the goodness of mankind."</u>

-Anthony Fauci (this from an interview with 'the-scientist.com' in May 2003)

What is a 'humanist'? I'll let Encyclopedia Britannica start off:

Humanism, a system of education and mode of inquiry that originated in northern Italy during the 13th and 14th centuries and later spread through continental Europe and England. The term is alternatively applied to a variety of Western beliefs, methods, and philosophies that place central emphasis on the human realm.

Humanism emphasizes humans and human society as the most important thing in life, not the supernatural/God/Jesus.

This is exactly an atheist point of view of the world, and the view that the proponents of the New World Order prefer you had over faith in God. It's a belief that human needs and values are more important than religious beliefs, and should take precedence.

I'm sure shuttering all the churches and the arrests of clergymen and parishioners put a smile on Fauci's face. I've researched Fauci and found not one reference to his belief in, or worship of, Jesus. Plenty of talk about being educated by Jesuits though...**and how they profoundly influenced him.**

I wonder if Fauci has taken the Jesuits' Extreme Oath of Induction? Someone should ask him!!

Humanists are typically of the mantra 'if it feels good do it' or more accurately 'do what thou wilt shall be the whole of the law' ala Aleister Crowley.

They are pro-LGBTQ lifestyle, pro-abortion, pro-transhumanism, pro-genetically modifying anything possible, along those lines. Basically, science and everything it can do for humanity is your god, just as the NWO teaches. After all, science and everything it can do is going to bring their god back to life, King Nimrod, and he's arguably alive right this second but we'll save that for another update.

Here's something with too much detail to get into here and is for you to follow up on: A former colleague of Dr. Fauci who had a falling out with him, Dr. Judy Mikovits, has recently gone public and on record in interviews stating that it is her position that Dr. Fauci quashed evidence she had about the HIV epidemic years ago that resulted in MILLIONS OF DEATHS WORLDWIDE. If what she was saying wasn't true, she could be sued but then all the facts would come out in court and Fauci can't have that, so he slanders and stonewalls her.

Mikovits' character has since been assassinated by the mainstream media and others but if you listen to everything that happened without blinders you will see that she is telling the TRUTH and has been vilified for it because it paints Fauci in an unfavorable light.

The mainstream media is currently in the process of trying to build Fauci up to be a hero for what's coming with the second wave of COVID-19....the 'mutated' version they will release later this year.

The press right now is calling him 'America's Doctor' and pushing him up the pop-culture ranks by showcasing all the mugs, bobbleheads, etc. referencing this new American hero.....*gag*

I've read up on this Fauci-guy. He was alleged by many to be a tyrant in his department at the NIH, bullying underlings, firing them if they had research he wanted to claim for his own, he owns many vaccine-related patents, etc. If this guy was pro-humanity why is he patenting anything? I've seen that him and Gates stand to make BILLIONS OF DOLLARS off this upcoming COVID-19 vaccine.

So not only are all the Gates' card-carrying socialist globalist liberals, it appears that ol' Tony is too...and now he's in the driver's seat to help this whole thing blow up in Trump's face and excuse his 'losing' the upcoming election.

In emails released by Wikileaks in 2016, there is an email from Anthony Fauci to Cheryl Mills, a top Clinton aide at the time, on the date Hillary Clinton testified about Bengazi, January 23, 2013. Now we all know from looking into it that Hillary is GUILTY of TREASON and directly responsible for the deaths of four United States citizens among other alleged actions that came out of Benghazi...she's a guilty, treasonous piece of crap worthy of a knotted rope!

Fauci had watched the hearing earlier in the day and sent the following email intending his well-wishes to be passed on to Killary:

Cheryl:

Anyone who had any doubts about the Secretary's stamina and capability following her illness had those doubts washed away by today's performance before the Senate and the House. She faced extremely difficult circumstances at the Hearings and still she hit it right out of the park. Please tell her that we all love her and are very proud to know her.

Warm regards,

Tony

This was just the text of the email, all other info from it was removed by yours truly but is online if you look.

Now, Fauci has been head of the NIH's National Institute of Allergy and Infectious Diseases since 1984....36 years!!

I cannot find any evidence or documentation anywhere that shows that Fauci has petitioned the NIH, the WHO, the Congress or any of the handful of Presidents that he served under that we needed to establish some kind of 'pandemic panel' or 'pandemic task force' or anything of the sort. Don't you think as the number 1 guy on the topic that he should have been clamoring for action....**KNOWING THAT A PANDEMIC WAS NOT A MATTER OF IF BUT WHEN?????**

Instead of telling us all to prepare against a coming pandemic, he was busy creating patents for vaccines that could be sold in a pandemic to make him and others money, namely Gates & co.

We've spent TRILLIONS on 'national defense' but not a damn DIME on preparing for a pandemic? They left us wide open for this false flag to destroy the United States...INTENTIONALLY!!

Even after the United States and the world had bouts with SARS, Ebola, etc. there wasn't a peep from this guy about what to do to prepare.

This whole thing has been long in planning, way pre-Trump. I've read a ton of info on Fauci and he is always adamant that he doesn't involve politics in his actions or thought-processes...BULLSH!T. He sent a memo to support Hillary right from his government-sanctioned office...surely on government time!!! OUR TIME!!

He is a TOTAL PLANT so watch out, especially in light of Event 201 that you should have looked into by now from my last report. Oh, you didn't look into it? That's fine, I got you fam...

Event 201: A Global Pandemic Exercise

That's exactly what is was called folks, "A Global Pandemic Exercise" and it took place on October 18, 2019. This was a simulation of a coronavirus pandemic that would go on for 18 months and go on to kill 65 million people globally.

This was an 18-month simulation crammed into a 3.5 hour presentation that you yourself can watch on YouTube as of the publishing of this update report.

It was orchestrated (of course) and sponsored by (of course again) the Bill and Melinda Gates Foundation, Johns Hopkins University, and the World Economic Forum.

The purpose of this simulation was basically to try and gauge what would happen to the world and society if a pandemic hit being as unprepared as we were. They were essentially testing the water to see if the time was right to pull the trigger on this false flag.

It was.

A mere 10 weeks after this simulation, the first cases of COVID-19 started showing up in force in Wuhan, China. That means the virus would have been released at least 3-4 weeks ahead of it becoming a threat by showing up in noticeable numbers....which means it was released about 6 weeks after Event 201! Not a coincidence in my book!!! This is like 9/11 all over with so many 'coincidences' that the circumstantial evidence is stacking up like cord wood against these bastards.

Now, you've read my first book, you know all about 9/11 and that false flags are what scores the most points in the NWO vs. Humanity fight we're in and always have been. This time they are going for the jugular though, no more messing around. If you've got an OUNCE of FIGHT in you, sentinel, it's going to be now or NEVER to save our country, I will hold out hope until the bitter end for our country and our kids' future.

I'm not even joking here. This is THE EVENT that David Rockefeller spoke of....remember?

"We are on the verge of a global transformation. All we need is the right major crisis and the nations will accept the New World Order."

-David Rockefeller, Statement to the United Nations Business Council, September 23, 1994

Now why do you suppose that Rockefeller uttered those words at a business meeting in particular? And why was 1/3 of the parties involved with Event 201 a globalist business organization that is completely pro-NOW, The World Economic Forum. What do they have to do with a pandemic? Oh that's right, the financial Armageddon and Greatest Depression that would go along with a huge pandemic...which we don't really have just yet, but will soon.

The damage has already been done to the economy. Like I said in the first update book, we took a gut shot and are on a slow bleed-out...wandering through the woods like a hapless, doomed deer....we're going on adrenalin at this point.

The Federal gooberment just keeps borrowing money and throwing it at us and all over the place and the 'recession' hasn't even started yet!!

Now it sounds like they are going to throw trillions more dollars at the population to keep everyone semi-appeased as this thing goes off the rails.

God help us....there is an unbelievable storm coming.

The globalists know our highly-interconnected way of society these days can't take a jolt to the system like it did. You think things are bad now with so many out of work, and we have TP and meat shortages occurring right now, you just wait for what's coming later this year. I'm afraid this is going to get ugly.

I can't emphasize enough to be prepping like mad right now with everything you've got. I'm so sorry to be saying all this downer-crap but dammit I am PISSED OFF!!!! I actually DO give a crap about you and our country, not Gates who wants to help push us under.

They are killing our country right as you are reading this-you've got to help!

You've got to research NOW and speak intelligently to others on what's going on. If we fail, we're DONE. SOMEONE HAS GOT TO STOP BILL GATES AT ALL COSTS. BARRING SOMETHING ILLEGAL WE HAVE SOCIAL MEDIA FOR NOW SO USE IT BEFORE WE LOSE IT!! STRENGTH IN NUMBERS...WAKE PEOPLE UP NOW!!!!!!

Right now, I am in TIME OUT on Facebook where I'm a notorious troublemaker but YOU PROBABLY AREN'T ON THEIR RADAR LIKE ME SO TIME TO THROW DOWN SENTINEL!

GET ON SOCIAL MEDIA AND START CONNECTING TO OTHER TRUTHERS! START YOUR OWN TRUTHER PAGES! WHEN YOU NETWORK WITH OTHER TRUTHERS THERE ARE INDEPENDENT FACTUAL NEWS ARTICLES GALORE AND MEMES YOU CAN SHARE WITH SLEEPING FRIENDS AND FAMILY!

LOOK ON INSTAGRAM, FACEBOOK, ~~MYSPACE~~ SNAPCHAT, WE'RE EVERYWHERE ALL UP IN THE NWO'S GRILLE!!!!!! COME ON!!!!! 😊

Ok....I'm settled now. Geez, what a bunch of crap my friend. I seriously had hoped we had another 20-30 years before this so maybe we did our job too well and their AI told them that if they didn't move now that they would be HUNG from tall trees! I still hold out hope for that actually!!

Anyways, that's Event 201 in a nutshell.

Now about this microchip business.....GRRRRRRRR!!!!!!!!!!!!

ID2020, yet ANOTHER of Bill Gates' babies...another piece of this false flag puzzle we're working out. You're gonna love this.

The ID2020 ALLIANCE

"I've got an interesting story to tell you now. There was a man named Aaron Russo, a very patriotic American who has since passed away. Mr. Russo made one of the best documentaries of all time about the New World Order agenda entitled "America: Freedom to Fascism", and I highly recommend you see it. It is available, for free, on youtube.com as of the printing of this book.

Aaron Russo was an acclaimed Hollywood producer who made the movies "Trading Places" (Eddie Murphy/Dan Akroyd) and "The Rose" (Bette Midler) among other big-name successful movies. He got into a disagreement with the IRS over some issues, which were complete BS on the part of the IRS after I learned the background facts of his story. To vent his anger he made a movie called "Mad as Hell" slamming them. Nicholas Rockefeller, son of current Rockefeller family kingpin and "head" of the American branch of the Illuminati David Rockefeller, found the movie intriguing, and after learning Russo was a big roller in Hollywood, decided he wanted to meet Aaron. The two met and became very close friends very quickly, with the friendship lasting for a few years. During this time, and approximately 11 months before 9/11 happened, Nicholas revealed to Aaron Russo the entire New World Order plan, that they were trying to implement a one world government ran by the banking industry, of which the Rockefellers are intricately part of, as you now know.

Russo, being the truly patriotic American he was, was horrified to learn the details about this, but he knew Rockefeller was telling him the truth. He ended their friendship over this information, and then went public with it after Nicholas' prophecy about 9/11 came to pass. According to Russo, Rockefeller's words on 9/11 were something along the lines of "There is going to be an event soon. We're going to invade Afghanistan and our troops will be looking for terrorists in caves over there, and then we're going to invade Iraq." Remember now, Russo says that Rockefeller told him this months in *advance of 9/11, and it all came to pass exactly as he had said. You can hear and see Russo speak about this on a handful of clips on youtube.com.*

He didn't tell Russo exactly what the event was, but it is not hard to deduce when he tells of the end result of it. He also foretells of the coming "war on terror" and how it is going to be a farce but the Mainstream Media will convince the people that it is real, and that the coming "event" is going to enable the federal government to take more and more of our liberties and freedom away. Rockefeller also revealed that they were behind the formation of the European Union, and that they were trying to form the North American Union next, by which the United States, Canada and Mexico would form a borderless community. The ultimate goal, according to Rockefeller, was to implant all people of the world with RFID chips, and have all of your money and personal information contained in these chips, which they would control through the banking system that they (Illuminati) owned."

-From my first book, "Rise of the New World Order 1: The Culling of Man", released January of 2013, *Chapter 11/J: The 9/11 Truth Movement:*

"**The ID2020 Alliance**"…that's what they are calling their little sheeple-branding project.

Sounds inviting, doesn't it? Sounds like something you want to be part of, no?

Probably not, especially after I get done with them here…*cracks knuckles*

To start with, this is a United Nations-founded project. So…the one world government predicted by the Bible is in place, the United Nations, and now they are pushing a global digital ID to track every human on the planet.

Perfect.

I don't like Wikipedia, but this is good for what we need it for…in fact REALLY good lol…make sure you click on the hyperlink 'Sustainable Development Goal' of Agenda 2030 to see what the digital ID is going to try to help them accomplish:

History: In May 2016, at the United Nations Headquarters in New York, the inaugural ID2020 summit brought together over 400 people to discuss how to provide digital identity to all, a defined Sustainable Development Goal including to 1.5bn people living without any form of recognized identification. Experts in blockchain and other cryptographic technology joined with representatives of technical standards bodies to identify how technology and other private sector expertise could achieve the goal.

In 2019, ID2020 started a new digital identity program in collaboration with the government of Bangladesh and vaccine alliance Gavi.

Mission: ID2020 is a public-private consortium in service of the United Nations 2030 Sustainable Development Goal of providing legal identity for ***ALL*** people, including the world's most vulnerable populations.

United Nations' Agenda 2030's Sustainable Development Goal 16.9: *"provide legal identity to all, including birth registration, by 2030"*

This ID system **WILL** be rolled out, in the third world to start with, but once it's established as the 'norm' it will be forced onto the first world countries.

Surprise...surprise... The Rockefeller Foundation provided the seed money to get ID2020 going with the UN they contributed the land for, founded and continue to participate in controlling today. The project's other members include Gavi the Vaccine Alliance (Gates), Microsoft (Gates), Accenture (Microsoft/Gates business partner in other ventures) and IDEO.org (Rockefeller and Gates Foundation partner).

So this ID2020 is full-on Rockefeller incepted-and-directed, Gates-implemented, and it IS the one world digital ID that is coming so you better brush up on it even more than what I'm relating here. This is going to be connected to the global digital currency that will come about after the death of the fiat United States dollar and the rest of the nations' fiat currencies.

This new digital ID is going to come in as a 'necessary evil' to track who has had COVID-19, who has been vaccinated and against what 'mutations' of COVID-19....this crap is just beginning people, and we'll watch it all unfold together, right before our eyes.

They are using COVID-19 as a false flag trojan horse to get everyone tracked...by their system. At first the third world and 'volunteers' were targeted but then after more and more sign on the pressure will begin to get everyone into their system. Now they have an excuse to just go full-bore at humanity with this thanks to the convenience of this plannedemic.

The World Economic Forum is also involved with ID2020...the exact same WEF who participated in Event 201!

Now this from the ID2020 website's home page:

"**We** need to get digital ID right. Identity is vital for political, economic, and social opportunity. But systems of identification are **_archaic, insecure, lack adequate privacy protection_**, and for over a billion people, inaccessible. Digital identity is being defined now-and **we** need to get it right."

Now, where it says _'we'_ they don't mean you and me and them friend, they mean themselves, the globalist NWO cabal pushing this global digital ID.

Notice how they make out their system to be the only logical choice as all other systems are 'archaic, insecure and lack privacy protection'. **_You'll surely never be safer than with the ID2020 Alliance_**...*rolls eyes*

This is from the ID2020 website's 'overview' page:

"ID2020 is coordinating funding for identity and channeling those funds toward high-impact projects, enabling diverse **_stakeholders_** - UN agencies, NGOs, governments, and enterprises - to pursue a coordinated approach that creates a pathway for efficient and responsible implementation **_at scale._**"

Well, surely the **stakeholders** want their owned property to be kept track of.

Don't farmers tag their cattle as soon as they are born? I live in the middle of cattle country and you better believe they do! Now they want to brand their sheep...how thoughtful, they didn't want us to get lost...or more likely they want to know where you are 24/7 to make sure you get all your upcoming vaccines!

I could list quote after quote from the ID2020 website but I'll leave you just one more, from their FAQ page. You yourself should snoop through their site also and often as it's going to be changing as events unfold.

"What is a "good" digital identity?"

A "good" digital identity is one that is truly yours. With a "good" digital identity you can enjoy your rights to privacy, security, and choice...(*insert laugh track HERE*)

The right to privacy is the right to permission access to your information at a granular level on an ongoing basis. Today, we consent once to give access to our digital identifiers. While it is possible in some digital spaces to revoke consent, revocation mechanisms are often esoteric and hidden behind high barriers to entry. True privacy means that you control access to individual digital identifiers, and that you can revoke (or modify) that access easily, at any time.

The right to security is all about protecting your data from unwanted access. Our certified digital identity systems must adhere to the highest security standards in existence today. And we are constantly evolving our Technical Requirements, which you can view here, in response to a changing landscape.

Last but not least, the right to choice is essential, and often overlooked in the digital world. Though you certainly have the right to choose among a few providers, and to exchange access to your information for that right, __true choices are few and far between in the digital world; to get philosophical for a moment, what freedom actually exists in a world of prescribed,__

circumscribed choices? A world that, in most cases, takes a certain kind of
digital presence as a given?

Achieving each of these rights depends on shifting the locus of control away
from institutions and towards you.

A "good" digital identity is one that is portable, persistent, privacy-protecting,
and personal.

Portability means that your information can be moved seamlessly from
one hosting/storage site to another, without duplication, modification,
or deletion. Persistence refers to durability; that your digital identity will
stay with you for life, and that no individual or institution can duplicate,
modify, or delete it. Privacy-protection refers to the safeguards in place to
ensure that activities that you do not consent to are strictly forbidden.
Personal means that you control your information at a granular level on an
ongoing basis.

In short, a "good" digital is yours.

Basically, what I'm gathering from the above, is that the new digital
ID they are proposing is mobile, is on or in you at all times, and works in
conjunction with your biometrics/fingerprint/retina scanner/whatever. So
some type of digital tracker/storage device…like an RFID chip…will work
in conjunction with biometrics to confirm it really is you, anywhere on the
globe, without an ID like a driver's license or passport you have to carry
around. This will also control the digital global currency that is coming…I
wonder if "Baal" Gates is involved with that?

Oh wait, what's this? Microsoft just applied for a patent for their proposed
cryptocurrency (digital currency), patent # wo/2020/060606. Please take
special note of the last set of numbers…. If I didn't know any better (!) I'd say
the patent number looks like 06 06 06 …666…perfect. Thanks Baal Gates,
thanks a lot you ol' devil you.

Let's cut this ID2020 off here or I'll go on forever…up to you to look into
this further.

So much to know and so little time, that's why I'm doing what I'm doing for you, friend: Gathering the most pertinent info I can find on the most pressing topics the pedo-Satanists are up to and putting it all together.

Truly nothing is hidden, either deliberately or unintentionally, if you have the will to stomach what you might find. The truth is truly stranger than fiction in today's world.

Predictive Planning 101

"Vaccines, for Bill Gates, are a strategic philanthropy that feeds his many vaccine-related businesses (including Microsoft's ambition to control a global vac ID enterprise) and gives him dictatorial control over global health policy—the spear tip of corporate neo-imperialism"
-Robert F. Kennedy Jr. (Bobby's son!)

Just as uncle JFK had done, RFK Jr. is going up against the NWO/Deep State and needs us!

There are millions of people waking up to the vaccine agenda, including a handful of Hollywood stars, and even some whose kids have been vaccine injured including Robert DeNiro. In fact, DeNiro and Kennedy have teamed up to offer $100,000 to anyone who could conclusively prove that vaccines are safe!!

This whole forced-vaccine issue is coming so you need to be as informed as possible of the FACTS my friend.

It is a documented FACT that Gates and co. have been beating the drum of an imminent pandemic for about a decade. A global death-pandemic only comes around every 100 years-ish, so how could they have known, hmmmmmmmmmm???

The warnings issued by those in the know before and after this ongoing "pandemic" tip their hand, they knew this was coming because they had a hand in causing it.

Let's start with Fauci...you tell me how it's even believable that someone could issue an imminent warning for a 'surprise' outbreak of pandemic?

"If there's one message that I want to leave with you today based on my experience, it is that there is no question that there will be a challenge to the coming administration (Trump) in the arena of infectious diseases.... No matter what, history has told us definitively that [outbreaks] will happen," he said. "It is a perpetual challenge. It is not going to go away. The thing we're extraordinarily confident about is that we are going to see this in

the next few years.... The mistake that so many people have made ... is a failure to look beyond our own borders in the issue of the globality of health issues, not only things that are there that will come here but surprises that we'll have... We will definitely get surprised in the next few years"

-Dr. Anthony Fauci, speaking in 2017 at the "Pandemic Preparedness in the Next Administration" at the Georgetown University Medical Center just a few days before Trump was sworn in, January 2017.

Now on to Bill Gates...

Gates has been warning the world about a dangerous pandemic since 2010. Has he been hounding the federal government since then to prepare? No. It's been all lip service, just a casual comment here and there about getting prepared so he could say 'I told you so' right about now. If I was Gates, I would have held multiple high-level meetings and pounded the point home that we weren't ready and to get prepared, but no, he instead has spent his billions for after-the-fact treatments, aka vaccines. That's where the money's at, not trying to head off a disaster.

The H1N1 flu strain got a lot of attention in 2009. Most of the headlines made it sound dangerous. Early in the epidemic we thought that a very high percentage of infected people were getting sick, and it was quite scary.

But the real story isn't how bad H1N1 was. The real story is that we are lucky it wasn't worse because we were almost completely unprepared for it.

When an epidemic breaks out, there are four steps to try to contain it. The first is to gather data about the disease—where it is and how it is spreading. Second is to limit the movement of people from place to place—with quarantine a last option. Once a disease is widespread this is very hard to do. Third is to have drugs of some type that reduce how much someone infects others and that reduces the severity of the sickness. Fourth is to make a vaccine that is effective against the disease and give it to anyone who is at risk.

We did a reasonable job of gathering data, partly due to the capacity that had been set up to track avian flu. But for all the other steps, we didn't manage to do anything that would have stopped a serious epidemic. In other words, the modest death toll from this flu epidemic is entirely because we were lucky.

Hopefully this outbreak will serve as a wakeup call to get us to invest in better capabilities, because more epidemics will come in the decades ahead and there is no guarantee we will be lucky next time....

- 'A Better Response to the Next Pandemic', from Gates' personal blog, January 19, 2010

Now this from his 2015 TED speech, titled *'The Next Outbreak? We're not ready"*:

"...So next time, we might not be so lucky (talking about the Ebola outbreak in 2014). You can have a virus where people feel well enough while they're infectious that they get on a plane or they go to a market. The source of the virus could be a natural epidemic like Ebola, or it could be bioterrorism.

So there are things that would literally make things a thousand times worse...But in fact, we can build a really good response system. We have the benefits of all the science and technology that we talk about here.

We've got cell phones to get information from the public and get information out to them.

We have satellite maps where we can see where people are and where they're moving.

We have advances in biology that should dramatically change the turnaround time to look at a pathogen and be able to make drugs and vaccines that fit for that pathogen...

We need to do simulations, germ games, not war games, so that we see where the holes are. The last time a germ game was done in the United States was back in 2001, and it didn't go so well.

So far the score is germs: 1, people: 0...

Now I don't have an exact budget for what this would cost, but I'm quite sure it's very modest compared to the potential harm.

The World Bank estimates that if we have a worldwide flu epidemic, global wealth will go down by over three trillion dollars and we'd have millions and millions of deaths...

There's no need to panic. We don't have to hoard cans of spaghetti or go down into the basement. But we need to get going, because time is not on our side..."

Now from 2016, the BBC interview with Slow Kill Bill...

"There's a lot of discussion right now about how we respond in an emergency, how we make sure that the regulatory and liability and organizational boundaries don't slow us down there, so I cross my fingers all the time that some epidemic like a big flu doesn't come along in the next 10 years"

This from a CBS news interview in 2017 at the 2017 World Economic Forum in Davos, Switzerland:

"The impact of a huge epidemic, like a flu epidemic, would be phenomenal because <u>all the supply chains would break down</u>. There'd be a lot of panic. Many of our systems would be overloaded, but being ready for epidemics of different sizes, there's a lot more we should do."

Also in 2017 at the Munich Security Conference in Munich, Germany:

"...When I decided 20 years ago to make global health the focus of my philanthropic work, I didn't imagine that I'd be speaking at a conference on international security policy. But I'm here today because I believe our worlds are more tightly linked than most people realize...

It's also true that the next epidemic could originate on the computer screen of a terrorist intent on using genetic engineering to create a synthetic version of the smallpox virus ... or a super contagious and deadly strain of the flu.

The point is, we ignore the link between health security and international security at our peril.

Whether it occurs by a quirk of nature or at the hand of a terrorist, epidemiologists say a fast-moving airborne pathogen could kill more than 30 million people in less than a year. And they say there is a reasonable probability the world will experience such an outbreak in the next 10-15 years.

It's hard to get your mind around a catastrophe of that scale, but it happened not that long ago. In 1918, a particularly virulent and deadly strain of flu killed between 50 million and 100 million people.

You might be wondering how likely these doomsday scenarios really are. The fact that a deadly global pandemic has not occurred in recent history shouldn't be mistaken for evidence that a deadly pandemic will not occur in the future.

And even if the next pandemic isn't on the scale of the 1918 flu, we would be wise to consider the social and economic turmoil that might ensue if something like Ebola made its way into a lot of major urban centers. We were lucky that the last Ebola outbreak was contained before it did.

The good news is that with advances in biotechnology, new vaccines and drugs can help prevent epidemics from spreading out of control. And, most of the things we need to do to protect against a naturally occurring pandemic are the same things we must prepare for an intentional biological attack.

First and most importantly, we have to build an arsenal of new weapons—vaccines, drugs, and diagnostics.

Vaccines can be especially important in containing epidemics. But today, it typically takes up to 10 years to develop and license a new vaccine. To significantly curb deaths from a fast-moving airborne pathogen, we would have to get that down considerably—to 90 days or less.

We took an important step last month with the launch of a new public-private partnership called the Coalition for Epidemic Preparedness Innovations. The hope is that CEPI will enable the world to produce safe, effective vaccines as quickly as new threats emerge.

The really big breakthrough potential is in emerging technology platforms that leverage recent advances in genomics to dramatically reduce the time needed to develop vaccines.

This is important because we can't predict whether the next deadly disease will be one we already know, or something we've never seen before...

Of course, the preventive capacity of a vaccine won't help if a pathogen has already spread out of control. Because epidemics can quickly take root in the places least equipped to fight them, we also need to improve surveillance...

The third thing we need to do is prepare for epidemics the way the military prepares for war. This includes germ games and other preparedness exercises so we can better understand how diseases will spread, how people will respond in a panic, and how to deal with things like overloaded highways and communications systems...

Imagine if I told you that somewhere in this world, there's a weapon that exists—or that could emerge—capable of killing tens of thousands, or millions, of people, bringing economies to a standstill, and throwing nations into chaos.

You would say that we need to do everything possible to gather intelligence and develop effective countermeasures to reduce the threat.

That is the situation we face today with biological threats. We may not know if that weapon is man-made or a product of nature. But one thing we can be almost certain of. A highly lethal global pandemic will occur in our lifetimes.

When I was a kid, there was really only one existential threat the world faced. The threat of a nuclear war.

By the late 1990s, most reasonable people had come to accept that climate change represented another major threat to humankind.

I view the threat of deadly pandemics right up there with nuclear war and climate change. Getting ready for a global pandemic is every bit as important as nuclear deterrence and avoiding a climate catastrophe...

When the next pandemic strikes, it could be another catastrophe in the annals of the human race. Or it could be something else altogether. An extraordinary triumph of human will. A moment when we prove yet again that, together, we are capable of taking on the world's biggest challenges to create a safer, healthier, more stable world."

Now on to 2018, Gates was giving multiple warnings to multiple sources all year, way too many quotes here, but he keeps hounding on the need for 'germ games' like war games to create simulations in anticipation of the real deal, which he did in late 2019 just 6 weeks before the pandemic began we are currently in!

Why in the HELL are Gates & co. running germ games and not our federal government? TRILLIONS spent on 'Homeland Security' since 9/11 and we weren't even prepared for something that was not a matter of if but when, even without NWO help?? Give me a break!!! We were INTENTIONALLY left wide open to what is happening now.

On February 28, 2020, Gates released an article he penned for the prestigious New England Journal of Medicine that you should read. I'll just give a couple of quotes from Gates here:

"In any crisis, leaders have two equally important responsibilities: solve the immediate problem and keep it from happening again. The Covid-19 pandemic is a case in point... Now we also face an immediate crisis. In the

past week, <u>Covid-19 has started behaving a lot like the once-in-a-century</u> <u>pathogen we've been worried about. I hope it's not that bad, but we should</u> <u>assume it will be until we know otherwise....</u>"

So, miraculously they predicted this pandemic, are saying it's the 'big one', have their hands in every piece of the pie to do with it, are at complete odds with nationalist/Republican Trump because the people behind this are globalist-elitist-pedo-Satanists and now they are telling us publicly that we are not done with this pandemic and it is coming back and things are going to be flat-out awful.

MOST viruses DO NOT COME BACK FOR A SECOND WAVE. How do they KNOW that this one is unless they are responsible! There are many things coming out of this pandemic in favor of the New World Order, but the big prize is blaming this whole economic/heath disaster on Trump so they can throw the election to the now-party-of-the-NWO....the (D) party. Again, the agenda for global enslavement by the proponents of the New World Order is a leftist, socialist agenda, which is why the battle lines are currently forming between mask-wearing sheep and anti-mask, pro-freedom patriots who know there is an agenda unfolding.

Remember, this current version of COVID-19 is not even as dangerous as the regular flu, the numbers have been completely inflated and there is chaos in all the numbers being reported...intentionally. Wait until the chaos hits of the second wave this Fall/Winter. When this laboratory-created 'mutation' hits, you will know who to go after with torches and pitchforks:

"There's a possibility that the assault of the virus on our nation next winter will actually be even more difficult than the one we just went through. And when I've said this to others, they kind of put their head back, they don't understand what I mean. We're going to have the flu epidemic and the coronavirus epidemic at the same time"
-CDC Director Robert Redfield in an interview with The Washington Post, April 21, 2020. Now he's predicting a flu pandemic to boot!!

"Lifting restrictions too quickly could lead to a deadly resurgence"
-World Health Organization Director General Tedros Adhanom Ghebreyesus, April 10, 2020

"It has a very dangerous combination and this is happening ... like the 1918 flu that killed up to 100 million people. But now we have technology, we can prevent that disaster, we can prevent that kind of crisis. Trust us. The worst is yet ahead of us. Let's prevent this tragedy. It's a virus that many people still don't understand."
-World Health Organization (WHO) Director-General Tedros Adhanom Ghebreyesus, April 20, 2020 (he's referencing vaccines btw to save us)

Both the CDC and the WHO and other 'experts' are saying that a second wave is on the way without knowing this for a fact, or do they? This is so when they release the new version Bill Gates will be on the teevee in his stupid sweater and smile smugly, shrug his shoulders and say "Told you so".

Now on to the predictive programming, and Netflix in particular....

On September 29, 2019, Netflix released *"Inside Bill's Brain: Decoding Bill Gates".*

This from the Netflix website about it: *Take a trip inside the mind of Bill Gates as the billionaire opens up about those who influenced him and the audacious goals he's still pursuing. Microsoft co-founder Bill Gates opens up about his childhood, business career and passion for improving the lives of people in the developing world.*

This is a 3-part 'investigative series' claims Netflix, but it's nothing of the sort. It's a 3-hour propaganda piece to try and make Gates look like an intelligent, caring philanthropist when he's really a diabolical, elitist eugenicist working for the Illuminati pedo-Satanists.

This was to plant the seed months before the pandemic ever appeared that Gates cares about humanity and is there to help us....HA!

Next we have *"Explained: The Next Pandemic"*, released November 7, 2019...about two months before the plannedemic we're now in the middle of and no end in sight.

This was filmed months before the 'pandemic' and even predicted the next pandemic would come out of a Chinese wet market, the current official story according to Gates, Fauci and co.

Gates himself starred in this and predicted a coming pandemic...**as he's done every year since 2015.**

Finally, from Netflix, the crown jewel of predictive programming of this pandemic, on January 22, 2020, they released *"Pandemic: How To Prevent an Outbreak"*, just as it was coming to light there was a novel coronavirus on the loose in China...allegedly turning into the pandemic of today.

This was filmed in 2018-2019.... many months ahead of the outbreak.

When you have an unusual amount of 'coincidences' they can ultimately be assembled as I have in this book into what is called 'circumstantial evidence'. There is not a single smoking gun—yet—that Gates had a hand in this plannedemic, but the evidence of too many coincidences are piling high at this point and we're not even close to done with him here

The Shutdown

There has **NEVER** been a quarantine over such an initially benign virus...**EVER**. That alone is a red flag to me that we are entering the false flag to end all false flags and bring in the full New World Order tyranny.

Look at how far we've fallen and so fast. So many unemployed. Mom and Pop companies going under left and right...including mine. Nobody wants me in their house on the eastside of Seattle...it's Libland! It's the land of the masked sheep now!!!

You know as well as I do that society always just powered through any flu pandemic in the past, which is what we **SHOULD** have done, so what is happening now is for an agenda to be certain.

So what has changed? It's time for the New World Order.

In the past, employees would just have to take their turn getting sick like we always used to. If enough employees got sick that company would shut down for a couple of weeks or whatever **ON THEIR OWN** and then get back to work at their own discretion. No laying anyone off. No government stimulus. Any of it.

Now we've got the co-opted gooberment shutting everything down for the NWO agenda. So many of the state governors are controlled it's not even funny, a lot of Masons and Jesuits I'm assuming...the Deep State/Illuminati's foot soldiers working towards the Secret Destiny of America, the New Babylon, which is burned in Revelation....that's us.

The whole plannedemic is working perfectly on many fronts.

People are afraid to use cash now because it could be "contaminated" with coronavirus, paving the way for the abolishment of cash in favor of a 'clean, digital currency' that can be 100% tracked by the Masters of the Great Plan.

Not that there will be much cash to spend anyways.

The economy isn't getting better, it's going right in the toilet. I cannot even understand why people are still in the stock market other than sheer greed. They will be sheared like the sheep they are; nothing can save them from what's coming.

Record numbers of people unemployed and more brutally bad numbers are coming in weekly and will continue to come.

Keep in mind/unemployment will start running out soon for a lot of people and there will be no jobs for them to go back to.

You thought there was division in politics before this pandemic, you ain't seen nuthin' yet.

Sides are being chosen now. People are tattling/turning each other in for violating rules that violate our Constitutional rights. See how easy that was? People wonder how a government can happen like that in the Soviet Union or Nazi Germany but your witnessing it unfold right now.

Welcome to the USSA.

It is largely the left-leaning that have chosen to take up with the state and turn into statists and report everyone...namely the free-thinking and conservative-value-minded people who are rebelling against the illusion of having lost their freedoms. You and I are smart enough to know we didn't have that much freedom even before this whole pandemic thing thanks to the Patriot Act, the NDAA, etc.

We are being constantly surveilled, all of our digital info goes into our files at NSA in Utah, and I mean EVERYTHING you do on your phone, computer, car...everything.

If you've read my first book you know that the New World Order conspiracy to enslave the world is a leftist, socialist conspiracy with Limousine Libtards at the top.

A Limousine Libtard is a liberal elitist who is involved in 'do as I say, not as I do' politics.

This not only includes Rothschilds and Rockefellers, it includes most of the Hollywood and entertainment elite---all certified leftists. People like Bono, Leonardo DiCaprio and Al Gore, zooming all over the planet on private jets to tell you how evil you are for even existing---even their own lib-followers, so they are throwing themselves on their swords and begging for a carbon tax to save the world from the people who own the companies causing all the destruction, which are largely owned by liberals!! UNREAL.

The Lib-sheep activists are the same ones clamoring for action on 'climate change' while they let global bioterrorists like Monsanto operate unchallenged for decades as well as chemtrails, fluoridated water, GMO foods, etc.

This mandatory mask wearing/social distancing for a virus no deadlier than the flu is to smother the world under the bureaucratic jackboot and put police in charge of enforcing unjust, unfair and oppressive actions which further divides the people between public and government.

If masks really worked why are they releasing all the inmates by the thousands? They are doing it to make room for patriots who are going to soon rebel, plus all the others who are going to straight up RIOT when their unemployment runs out and there are no jobs, not to mention what commodity might be in short supply in the coming weeks.

Why do Mom and Pop stores have to stay closed if the masks work? Why can you go to Walmart or Target but not Granny's Antique Store in your hometown? Most people don't even know that the masks don't protect you from getting COVID-19, they help to prevent YOU from spreading it if you have it and don't know it.

Even an N95 mask is basically a sneeze guard. Nothing short of a full-face respirator with filter cartridges...a gas mask...would protect you from a deadly virus.

So, this Covid Circus is kicking into high gear now. Our Washington state Goobernor Dimslee just announced he has hired 1,400 new 'contact tracers' to take everyone who has 'tested positive' for COVID-19 and grill them about who they were in contact with recently so the Goobernator can hunt them down and test them!

Have you seen how they do the test? They seriously shove a long q-tip up your nose and about 4-6 inches into your sinus cavity!

It won't be long now before **EVERYONE IN THE STATE NEEDS TO BE TESTED THANKS TO SIX DEGREES OF SEPARATION.**

Right now, governments are setting up what they are calling '<u>contact tracing</u>', which will sooner or later ensnare EVERYONE in their net.

Everything that is happening now is setting the stage for what's coming in a few months so people are used to government walking all over their rights, and that's the 'mutated' version of COVID-19. And <u>**THAT**</u> will pave the way for a compulsory vaccine.

I doubt Trump would enact a nationwide vaccine law, and that will be one more nail in his political coffin I'm afraid.

Mandating forced vaccination…that will be saved for Hillary to do. I'm still betting on Hillary somehow worming her way back into DC to help finish us off.

Now….about this upcoming ~~optional~~ ~~mandatory~~ **compulsory** vaccine issue…

The COVID-19 Mandatory Vaccine

"Pharma has 80 COVID vaccines in development, but Gates & Fauci pushed Moderna's "Frankenstein jab" to the front of the line. Scientists & ethicists are sounding alarms. The vaccine uses a new, untested, and very controversial experimental RNA technology that Gates has backed for over a decade. Instead of injecting an antigen & adjuvant as with traditional vaccines, Moderna plugs a small piece of coronavirus genetic code into human cells, altering DNA throughout the human body and reprograming our cells to produce antibodies to fight the virus. MRNA vaccines are a form of genetic engineering called "germ line gene editing". Moderna's genetic alterations are passed down to future generations. In January The Geneva Statement the world's leading ethicists and scientists called for an end to this kind of experimentation. Moderna has never bought a product to market, proceeded through clinical trials, or had a vaccine approved by FDA. Despite Gates' investments, the company, was teetering on bankruptcy with $1.5 billion debt before COVID. Fauci's support won the company an astonishing $483 million in federal funds to accelerate development. Dr. Joseph Bolen, Moderna's former R&D Chief, expressed shock at Fauci's bet."I don't know what their thinking was", he told CNN, "When I read that, I was pretty amazed". Moderna and Fauci launched federally-funded human trials on March 3rd in Seattle. Dr Peter Hotez warns of potentially fatal consequences from skipping animal studies. "If there is immune enhancement in animals, that's a show-stopper". Dr Suhab Siddiqi, Moderna's Ex-Director of Chemistry, told CNN, "I would not let the [vaccine] be injected in my body. I would demand: Where is the toxicity data?" Former NIH Scientist Dr. Judy Mikovits says its criminal to test MRNA vaccines on humans. "MRNA can cause cancers and other dire harms that don't surface for years."

-Robert F. Kennedy Jr, 5/2/20 on Instagram

At this point in our research, I shouldn't have to tell you about all the bad things that are floating around as adjuvants in the current vaccines for various diseases, that's a given. Just a smorgasbord of poison.

Before anyone even CONSIDERS forcing me to take a 'compulsory' vaccine to be a part of society, you better answer me these questions first:

- Why was a federal law passed in 1986 absolving ALL VACCINE MAKERS to be held harmless from liable if any of their vaccines hurt, maim or kill anyone who gets one?
- Tell me what's in the vaccine, every ingredient, every mechanism of that ingredient, every side effect of injecting this stuff right into my blood stream where it has direct access to my brain
- It is in fact safe? I want to see all phases of testing proving it is safe
- Does it really work? I want to see all phases of testing proving it works

You know as well as I, friend, that **NONE** of the above legitimate questions/concerns will be addressed regarding the upcoming COVID-19 vaccine. They're just going to ram it down our throat.

Looks like Big Pharma All-Star **Merck** is in the running for a COVID-19 vaccine.... perfect. What could go wrong?

You know, Merck? The same Merck who kept Vioxx on the market after they KNEW it was killing people? Yeah, **THAT** Merck! Their lawyers must have worked up a formula to figure out how much liability they could withstand before they started losing money by keeping Vioxx on the market. Turns out the number was 55,000 human deaths they could be sued over before Vioxx would become unprofitable. Those board members should have been HUNG FROM TALL TREES BY THE NECK.

It's fine, it's nothing really. What's 55,000 lives compared to the billions Baal Gates is going to try and eliminate coming right up.

He has already taken Harmageddon to dizzying new heights since marshalling himself up as Captain Jabbin' and carpet bombing the third world with intentionally harmful vaccines.

Let's see exactly what he's been up to for the last few years since 'retiring' from Microsoft to pursue "philanthropic" endeavors.

Bill Gates, a white, extreme leftist, elitist-eugenicist spending his own money to eradicate the third world brown and black people. I'm surprised he's not a GOD in the white supremacist community!!! Ugh....he is truly a demon in the flesh.

Gates funded GSK's experimental malaria vaccine that killed 151 African infants and caused paralysis, seizures and convulsions to 1,048 of the 5,049 children administered the vaccine...**that's a 20% serious side effect rate.**

In India, Gates experimental polio vaccine, which upped the standard schedule of 5 to **50** polio vaccine doses/injections PER CHILD, paralyzed 480,000 Indian children between 2000 and 2017.

In 2017 the WHO reluctantly admitted that the global polio explosion was predominately vaccine strain, **meaning it came from Gates' vaccines!!!**

WHERE IS THE MAINSTREAM MEDIA ON THIS AND OTHER ATROCITIES!!!! **It is estimated that in 2018, ¾ of all global polio cases were from Gates' vaccines.**

In 2014, Gates funded the experimental HPV vaccine on 23,000 unwitting and unwilling girls in India with a handful dying and 1,200 suffering side effects including autoimmune and fertility disorders. Indian government investigators charged that Gates-funded researchers committed atrocious ethical violations during the course of the trials including bullying parents, forging consent forms, and refusing medical care to the injured girls!! The case is now grinding it's way through India's Supreme Court.

Gates & co. supplied the WHO with billions and in turn they chemically sterilized millions of Kenyan women with a tetanus sterility formula vaccine!! You can't make this stuff up!!

Gates also funded Johns Hopkins University experiments that intentionally infected hundreds of Guatemalans with sexually transmitted diseases for drug and vaccine testing.

If Gates was running around the United States using us as guinea pigs like he has done in the third world he'd be pushing up daisies by now but instead the Deep State PROTECTS HIM by using the WHO/CDC/NIH/ etc. as fronts to shield him in the third world.

Ever hear of the Tuskegee Experiment? Look into **THAT** to see just what the people in charge of your health can pull on you!!

Gates has hijacked the WHO agenda away from those programs that would most benefit the Third World peoples in the fight against disease. You know, things like clean water, hygiene, good nutrition, healthy economy, etc.

Apparently, Gates thinks good health only comes from a syringe or he'd be funding everything I just listed equally as vaccines but no, it's all vaccines from Gates.

Gates appears gleeful on teevee in video clips I've seen lately about the prospect of vaccinating all of the USA and the world with his products which will make him billions more and also please his NWO masters.

On March 19, 2020, Gates posted up on Reddit that he proposed a digital certificate to identify those who have received the COVID-19 vaccination.

People who have been vaccinated would receive a 'quantum dot tattoo', which is "a bit of dye that is invisible to the naked eye" but that can be seen and read via infrared light. This 'tattoo' would store a digital file with your vaccine info---among other things like your bank account info---that could be read with a scanner or smart phone.

This particular tracking system was developed at MIT and funded by.......yup.....The Bill and Melinda Gates Foundation.

Listen to what Bill Gates/WHO/CDC/Etc. are saying because they are merely telling you what the game plan is.

"One of the questions I get asked the most these days is when the world will be able to go back to the way things were in December before the coronavirus pandemic. My answer is always the same: when we have an almost perfect drug to treat COVID-19, or when almost every person on the planet has been vaccinated against coronavirus.

The former is unlikely to happen anytime soon. We'd need a miracle treatment that was at least 95 percent effective to stop the outbreak. Most of the drug candidates right now are nowhere near that powerful. They could save a lot of lives, but they aren't enough to get us back to normal.

Which leaves us with a vaccine.

Humankind has never had a more urgent task than creating broad immunity for coronavirus. Realistically, if we're going to return to normal, we need to develop a safe, effective vaccine. We need to make billions of doses, we need to get them out to every part of the world, and we need all of this to happen as quickly as possible.

That sounds daunting, because it is. Our foundation is the biggest funder of vaccines in the world, and this effort dwarfs anything we've ever worked on before. It's going to require a global cooperative effort like the world has never seen. But I know it'll get done. There's simply no alternative."
-Bill Gates, April 30, 2020 on his blog

So...that's what's going on in the world of Plannedemic 2020, starring Baal Gates, Crime Boss Fauci, the clowns at the WHO and CDC, and a host of other characters who will reveal themselves in due time...I'll be waiting.

Conclusion

Now, let's put my 15,000+ hours of NWO-research to good use and try and figure out what's coming so we can best prepare ourselves on all fronts.

The HUGE block of people who lost their jobs in the restaurant/hospitality industries and many other will exhaust their 26 weeks/6-7 months or whatever it is of unemployment right around August-September.... about the time I'm guessing for the appearance of the 'mutated' version of COVID-19 to really screw us.

This Depression is just getting started and I do not believe we're coming out of it so batten down the hatches NOW. Don't spend money on anything you don't have to...but wait! What's this???

Looks like there is more 'stimulus' gooberment cheese coming...just to keep the sheep appeased enough not to rebel while they set up the martial law infrastructure....contact tracing anyone?

I saw some numbers floating around lately...$2,000 per person per month and another $2,000 per child as long as there is pandemic-related hardship??? Sure! Just put it on the tab...OMG. This is just insanity.

The economy will be in such a shambles later this year, and with food shortages, riots, quarantine stir-craziness and general civil unrest that the sheep will **CRY** for a vaccine to make it all better...it will only make it worse once the NWO's foot is in the door to forced medical procedures.

Gates already said he wants death panels installed via the health system to determine if your life is worth saving when you are older and a 'burden' to society.

"...spending a million dollars on that last three months of life for that patient or laying off ten teachers. But that's called the death panel and you're not supposed to have that discussion..."
-Bill Gates, speaking at the 2010 Aspen Ideas Festival, Aspen, Colorado.

As I said in my first update, I'm looking at the pandemic and Trump's response to it to be blamed by the left for the financial woes coming. Trump will be blamed for the beginning of the Greatest Depression, not the Fed and the bought-and-paid-for corrupt Establishment politicians where the blame really belongs!!

And the media will sell it and the sheep will eat it up so between that and the proposed mail-in voting this will probably be the end of Trump's Presidency.

If we didn't have an overleveraged credit-economy backed up by nothing at all we wouldn't have so far to fall to hit the bottom of a depression but.... yeah. You've read my first book, you know what I'm talking about, we knew this was coming.

Trump will definitely be blamed for the societal meltdown coming over "his" virus response. The question is will he throw the patriots under the bus with a nationwide compulsory vaccine?

I'm no rocket scientist, but that would probably ignite a civil war. Forced vaccination is tantamount to medical rape and goes against the Geneva Convention not to mention our Constitution.

As we get closer to time to push for a compulsory vaccine, I'm expecting 1-3 mass shootings in close succession to shock the public into clamoring for gun control right before the vaccine becomes available so people can't resist it by shooting whoever is trying to jab them.

The recent mass shooting in Canada was the worst in their HISTORY and excused the immediate banning of 'assault rifles' at least on paper, guns have been heavily restricted in Canada for years.

So.....what do we do? What does humanity do to stand against a mob of Satan-worshipping trillionaires who control our world looking to kill 90+% of us?

You gotta get **MAD!!**

You gotta get **MOTIVATED!!**

They are trying to kill your KIDS!

They are trying to kill your aged GRANDPARENTS!

And most of all, they are trying to kill YOU!

Our only chance is to wake up enough people to stop them COLD, and you do that by educating yourself about this false flag and then educating others.

Here's some ammo for you, sentinel:

A timeline of this false flag, starting in 2010:

- *1/19/10 Gates initiates his personal alarm of an oncoming global pandemic on his personal blog*

- *3/18/15 Gates beats the drum of an oncoming global pandemic at a TED talk*

- *5/20/16 United Nations initiates ID2020*

- *12/30/16 Gates issues another warning of an oncoming global pandemic in a BBC interview*

- *1/16/17 At this point, Gates now beating the drum __yearly__ of an oncoming global pandemic, this time at the World Economic Forum in Switzerland, the same WEF involved in Event 201 and ID2020.*

- *2/17/17 Gates again warns of an oncoming global pandemic at the Munich Security Conference in Munich, Germany*

- *6/20/19 Gates files for patent for __WO/2020/060606 "Cryptocurrency system using body activity data"__*

- *9/20/19 Netflix releases "Inside Bill's Brain: Decoding Bill Gates" This 'documentary' was made to build up the public perception of Gates*

- *10/19/19 Gates and co. run Event 201. What are the odds? One in a MILLION.*

- *11/7/19 Netflix releases "Explained: The Next Pandemic"*

- *11/15/19 CDC posts nationwide in all major cities they are looking to hire "Public Health Advisors for their quarantine program" They KNEW a pandemic was coming and didn't warn the American public.*

- *12/18/19 Many news outlets report on Gates' new vaccine-tattoo technology, the Quantum Dot Digital Tattoo*

- 12/31/19 COVID-19 spreading at this point through Wuhan, China, having somehow (!) been let loose weeks before
- 1/21/20 First COVID-19 case shows up in the USA in Washington State
- 1/22/20 Netflix releases "Pandemic: How to Prevent an Outbreak"
- 2/28/20 Gates releases article in NEJM stating that COVID-19 is looking like a once-in-a-century pandemic and that we should assume it is until proven otherwise.
- 3/19/20 Gates posted up on Reddit that he is proposing a digital certificate to identify those who have received the COVID-19 vaccination
- 3/26/20 Gates receives patent for WO/2020/060606 "Cryptocurrency system using body activity data"
- 3/27/20 First Federal Government stimulus package signed into law, the CARES Act. They've been adding to this ever since, throwing trillions upon trillions at the economy trying to keep its head above water. Now they're talking about giving everyone monthly stipends. Ummm... when everyone is getting money from the government to live on, that's unadulterated socialism for those keeping score at home.
- 4/10/20 World Health Organization Director General Tedros Adhanom Ghebreyesus warns against lifting quarantine
- 4/18/20 Mainstream media announced that thousands of COVID-19 tests are actually contaminated from the factory with the virus that causes COVID-19. Anyone that got the test, arguably then got the disease!!! You can't make this shit up!!!
- 4/20/20 World Health Organization Director General Tedros Adhanom Ghebreyesus states "the worst is yet ahead of us"
- 4/21/20 CDC director Robert Redfield states that there will be a second wave of COVID-19 soon
- 4/24/20 Federal Government passes 4th pandemic stimulus package
- Also to note, in general throughout the timeline, fake news galore to push the false flag including showing mannequins on gurneys, never in modern

history has there been a quarantine and then the numbers were all wrong and the virus is less dangerous than the flu, ridiculous payouts from the feds to hospitals who diagnose/treat alleged COVID-19 sufferers motivating them to report false claims to get more money, nurses dancing on tiktok because there are bored with no patients to be attending to, numbers don't add up such as Tokyo, Japan having hardly any deaths while NYC is 'awash in deaths', youtube vids of actual doctors calling out this false flag and then censored/removed, tons of talk lately on mainstream media about the second wave, etc. etc. ad nauseum

- *Keep in mind the peculiarities about this plannedemic: we never closed the economy/country over such a benign illness before, economy has never sank so fast before in history, stimulus spending by the feds like never before in history and LIGHTNING FAST, we never were told we NEEDED A VACCINE IN ORDER TO GET LIFE BACK TO NORMAL before…EVER.*

If I was you, friend, here's what I would be doing:

Get out of the cities at all cost or at least try to make arrangements for a place to bug-out. You should be openly talking to friends and family about everything in this report and my books at this point because we are right there at the threshold of SHTF. I know this isn't an option for some of you, you're at the top of my prayers to be looked after. Just take solace in the fact that we're not here forever, only temporary, and there is no avoiding our physical death. I don't look forward to death, but I intend on prolonging it as long as possible! Everyone will pass at their particular apportioned time, no sense fretting about it.

You need to start talking in particular to your neighbors about this stuff, it's not conspiracy theory, it's conspiracy FACT and it's been in motion since 2,200 BC during the days of King Nimrod.

RESIST the NWO via fact-spreading on social media. I'm not advocating to go and march in the street at all, not at this time, not the ones who are truly awake. That just gets physical and ugly fast taking to the streets. We need our best and brightest sentinels on duty on the keyboard for right now, spreading truth.

Best for now, IMO, to go hard on social media with the facts that are in this report and in my books.

We are putting TREMENDOUS pressure on Gates in particular right now.

As of the publication of this report there are hundreds of thousands that have signed a petition to the White House to have Gates investigated for crimes against humanity!!!

YOU are your best defense against any virus they release. Your own immune system. And I'm not saying don't wear a mask. If it makes you feel better then that alone is worth it for your own piece of mind. You won't see me in one though. Again, only a full-face respirator can actually protect you like will be needed soon. All the more reason they are going to keep this quarantine-business going INDEFINITELY.

I've been studying up on how to home-remedy the COVID in my spare time (!). Zinc seems to be the best to take if you get it, or zinc-medicine like Zycam. Quinine is supposed to be helpful in working with the zinc to fight infection, it occurs naturally in tonic water so have that on hand to wash down your zinc pills.

I also have echinacea, goldenseal, turmeric, etc. on hand. Research the ins and outs of taking all of this stuff too, like you're not supposed to take zinc within an hour of a citrus beverage, etc.

Also, the taking of anti-inflammatories like ibuprofen could aggravate a COVID-19 infection. Lots to know and lots of time now under quarantine to research all of it my friend. High doses of vitamin C is also really good I hear, supposedly high dose IV vitamin C is how China got COVID-19 under control. Also Oregano Oil, Elderberry extract, apple cider vinegar pills, lots of water also to continually flush the body of toxins.

Without my faith I would be soooo lost right now, I pray every morning of every day.

I thank you for your support/book reviews my friends!!!! If we wake up enough people, we might be able to intimidate Gates and co. to stand down and back off this false flag, avoiding a second wave of pandemic. The damage has already been done though...I don't know if we can save the USA or not.

The rest of the world will largely cheer as we go down in flames and it's broadcast around the world, no one has farther to fall than us, and since 'we' bankrolled bombing the crap out of dozens of countries over the last few decades, they will rejoice at our self-destruction.

I'm sure Gates will ultimately be watching all this pandemonium that is coming unfold from the underground bunker at his house in Medina, Washington. Now THERE'S something for you to look into.

People have got to learn about Bill Gates. Print this report up and hand it out!!

I'll leave you for now with this excerpt from an article that appeared on CNBC on April 16, 2020:

"Amid the Covid-19 pandemic, people across the world have rushed to "panic buy" and stockpile food and toilet paper, fearing potential shortages.

But Bill and Melinda Gates began to stockpile food in their basement years before the current pandemic.

"A number of years ago, we talked about, 'What if there wasn't clean water? What if there wasn't enough food? Where might we go? What might we do as a family?' So, I think we should leave those preparations to ourselves," Melinda Gates told BBC Radio Live on Thursday.

"We had prepared, and had some food in the basement in case needed, and now we're all in the same situation," she said.

Hey, we're all in this together, right? Right…***rolls eyes***

Until next time my brother and sister sentinels….May YAH watch over you and yours and guide you as safely as possible down the treacherous path that 2020 is proving to be.

YAH bless.

-Jeff

RISE OF THE NEW WORLD ORDER: BOOK SERIES UPDATE AND URGENT STATUS REPORT VOL. 3

AUGUST 19, 2020

RIP David Dees

This has been the worst year ever for about everybody and this absolutely sucks but I'm afraid I'm going to have to begin this report with some truly sad news...damn.

Your friend and mine, David Dees, anti-NWO artist, activist extraordinaire and the cover artist for my books, passed away from the stage IV melanoma cancer I told you about in the first Update Report in March. He passed on May 31, 2020 at 62 years young in Oregon.

That dang Dees had an actively-growing, 3-inch black mole on his back for years and he never got it checked out. He didn't trust the medical establishment for anything and with good reason.

By the time the pain was so bad and he went in to the doctor to get it checked out it was way too late, the cancer had spread throughout his body.

He decided to forego traditional cancer therapies and tried the natural route to no avail, he was too compromised...and now he's gone.

I can't help but consider that Dees was intentionally taken out...perhaps zapped in the back with a DEW/Directed Energy Weapon of some sort by the evil ones to cause the cancer...I don't know. With his reach, he was surely one of their biggest enemies.

It came out in Congressional hearings in the 1970s that the CIA was running around with a 'heart attack gun' that shot a tiny ice bullet with deadly poison that would break down long before an autopsy could be performed. Perfect for taking out the enemies of the Great Plan. If you brought something like this up in today's world to the average sheep you would immediately be called a conspiracy theorist...and this was made public in US government proceedings decades ago!!

That was the 70s...we're talking about 40 years later. Who knows what kind of diabolical arsenal they have cooked up since then.

All I know for certain is he's gone and there is a HUGE hole not only in my heart but the Truth Community. No one has done more to shake and wake people up than Dees. He was just a gentle soul once you got to know him, but a tenacious warrior against the Great Plan.

I first met David online not long after I released my first book in January of 2013 but I had been a big fan and admirer of his since I first woke up in 2007.

His 'Ron Paul' artwork for the 2008 election drew me right to him and I still like to go back and look at all his old work like that, Dees was genius... just awesome art. He really was a super-patriotic guy too. He knew Ron Paul was our only hope and threw everything he had behind him.

So...my first book had this crappy-ass homemade cover that was all black with a white upside-down USA flag on the front of it when I first released my first book in January of 2013. I sent it to him to show him what I was currently using and he just laughed.

As he was working on the cover, he referred to it as 'that little black book' since the book was nearly all black except the writing and the flag...too funny to think back on that right now.

When I first sent it to him, the first book was called: **The Culling of Man: Rise of the New World Order**.

He said to me, "First thing we're doing is reversing the title". He went to work, reversed the title, and created the epic cover that you know today... thanks again Dees. What an honor to me to have him create an original piece of art—and a killer one at that---to help arm me against the NWO.

After I contacted him and he did my first book cover, I had some very interesting conversations on email with David about a variety of subjects, most notably showing me x-rays of his skull and showing where his tracking implant was from the ETs!! I didn't know what to think lol!

He'll always have a very special place in my memory...my heart. We didn't live very far away and I had plans to drive and meet him someday soon to talk in person about the third book cover...ugh. I wish I hadn't waited. What a year, right?

It was Dees' brazenness in going after the NWO/Great Plan agenda that helped to motivate me to cast aside any aversions I might have in deciding to go up against the global pedo-Satanic cabal by doing what I could to wake up the planet.

He selflessly gave away his art on one hand and lived hand-to-mouth on the other. He really did barely get by because he spent so much time fighting the NWO on his own time and dime. I donated money to him several times, telling him to 'get a pizza and a bottle of wine on me'.

I also gave him a couple good paying jobs, I paid him well for each of my two book covers. He loved it. He got to have fun making art, helped me, made some money, and fought the NWO all at once...perfect.

At least Dees is at peace now, no more pain, and won't have to go through the literal Hell on Earth coming right up, right? Right.

Someone had posted an image with a memorial on it right after he passed.

The second I saw it I grabbed it with the intention of using it here, now.

Thanks for all you did, brother David. Love you man.

Intro

Sorry this third update took so long to get out. I've been thinking on this particular update quite a bit so I can try to explain to those with eyes to see and ears to hear very clearly exactly what is being bombarded upon our country by the NWOwned mainstream media.

Our country is being whipped up against each other by their slick propaganda machine as if the controllers are trying to bring us to the brink of a new Civil War in the United States.

The 'left and right' have NEVER been further apart in our country's history.

No wonder they want to get rid of any evidence of the first Civil War, the Confederacy, the Confederate Flag, statues and any other reminders of the fact that we *already* butchered each other once by the skullduggery of the Illuminati bankers!!

If they get everyone at each other's' throats and then we have the riot-situation I see coming where it will be every man for himself....ugh.

I am absolutely heartbroken, disgusted and angry to see all my American brothers and sisters of all shades being force-fed lies about racism in the USA. And if it's not racism, it's pushing the NWO-pandemic narrative...or attacking Trump. That's it. That's the three main topics on the majority of the news/talk shows/etc. right now. I don't watch teevee remember, but you can't escape it on social media, the radio, friends, etc.

I've had a bunch of other stuff happening also that has been distracting me, keeping my head out of working on these updates/chapters for the upcoming third book.

You don't know how much I've been missing growing up a kid born in 1970. Life was so good in the 70s and 80s compared to these days with no cell phones, killer music, awesome movies, classic cars and **EVERYONE GOT ALONG GREAT.**

Heck! Being black in the 70s and 80s was super cool to me as a kid!

Do you have any idea how many tv shows, music, movies, etc. featured black people prominently? And they were EPIC.

In the 1970s it was like we were getting to know our black American brothers and sisters finally after shaking hands at the end of the 60s.

What happened to cause what's going on today? Oh yeah, the Great Plan... we're at the threshold of the culling of man, hence the subtitle of my first book. The rulers want absolute chaos in order to pull off this plannedemic-of-a-false-flag. They want us pointing fingers at each other instead of the evil ones pulling the levers.

Kids these days, and I'm talking about Millennials and Gen Z, have been brainwashed by the public-school indoctrination system like never before.

The angst against the 'system' started with the Baby Boomers in the 60s, accelerated with Gen X in the 80s and 90s until they went full-on socialism with the Millennials and Gen Z, wanting to change the 'system' completely.

They were taught that the USA is an evil, racist, capitalistic evil empire and that society is full of racists and bullies and boogeymen to invade their newly established "safe spaces". This is all part of the agenda to take the USA down and take us all into the End.

They are just now starting to get **EVERYONE** panicked, terrorized and full of hatred because they don't know how else to feel. This is all new to everyone, this pandemic/lockdown/quarantine/masks/social distancing/etc.

The panicked people don't know where to aim their frustration and coming anger over the whole situation.

This is all going to culminate with the persecution of Christians who are going to resist the RFID chip/Mark of the Beast to the death so be battle-ready, Christian Sentinels, because it's coming. I'm not going out on my knees, chipped like a dog and sure of my place in Hell if I let it happen.

Let's get right into this as time is short.

Where are we at in the plannedemic...

Well, the riots have begun I predicted in my first update and the protests and demonstrations in the cities are still going strong nightly over two and a half months since they began.

These are just the beginning of what's to come in terms of riots I'm afraid. You ain't seen nothin' yet.

The media is pushing mail-in voting and pushing it hard. I'm expecting it actually as that is the only way to ensure that Biden, Harris, Clinton or whoever gets into the driver's seat.

Let's see...what else has happened. Well the National Debt is up another $6 trillion. Just put it on the tab! And there is more spending coming.

Trying to spend your way out of the Greatest Depression of all time is going to cause hyperinflation, which explains why the precious metals markets are going ballistic. Gold and silver are good stores of wealth, but are worth nothing next to lead and the means to exchange that lead (!)

Fifty million workers have been laid off or furloughed. 60 million citizens went on food stamps. We've gone from 5% to 13+% unemployment.

The plannedmic has devastated the tourism/restaurant/hotel/hospitality businesses.

The service industry has been decimated by the lockdowns/quarantine. People no longer could wait to open and let the businesses go.

The government has threatened, fined and arrested church parishioners and their leaders.

All schools and colleges will be closed to in-person learning indefinitely, until there is a vaccine.

And then what? My kids aren't getting no Baal Gates poison injection. I'm making preparations right now for home-schooling, I will make it work!

Thousands and even millions of urgent surgeries for life-threatening conditions have been put on hold. You might be under quarantine but your cancer isn't.

I understand the suicide rate is spiking thanks to this BS quarantine business. This is for an illness that is not as dangerous as the flu, mind you. What are they going to do when the flu DOES come around? Are we supposed to wear masks for the rest of our lives? I don't think so!!

What is happening is another blatant false flag like 9/11 for the puppets in government to further trample what little liberty and freedom we had left.

And on. And on. And on. And on. And there is no sign of this letting up, only going to get worse going forward from here, every day ahead. Unless we wake up people in droves to the Great Plan and turn the tide.

Real pandemics don't rely on exaggerated virus models by Fauci and co., faulty testing kits, rigged results and falsified death certificates. Seems like no one is dying of flu this year, it's all covid-19...*rolls eyes*

This is a HISTORIC false flag and we are living in it right this second.

They are shutting the states back down again as I'm writing this. This means toilet paper manufacturers are soon to shut down again. Food manufacturers also will be shutting down again. I'm not going to tell you again that you should be prepping for what is coming down the line.

Now, if the various local governments were really serious about stopping the spread of covid shouldn't they have mandated masks months ago?

Kind of like taking a shit and THEN dropping your drawers, right? Right.

The mess has been made...allegedly. The people who are running the states' response to the plannedemic are either completely incompetent or in on the false flag, and I'm going with the latter!

People had to be slowly terrorized and broken in to the whole mask-thing. I know a mask isn't going to do anything to protect me from some 'deadly' virus, but if I don't wear one and I got 'mask shamed' I would lose my mind as I've got a terrible temper and the size to back it up! I need to stay OUT of jail lol...take that for what you will.

So, I literally AM wearing a mask for others' protection, not against the virus but so I don't stuff someone into a garbage can! What a jacked-up deal. I have asthma too so it really sucks. I just don't go out anymore...ugh.

Now throw in our current situation with **riots**/BLM/Antifa/'resurgence' of wave 1 of the plannedemic/financial markets acting irrationally as they are holding out the collapse for just the right moment for the mainstream media to pin it on Trump.

Since 1984 the stock market has predicted the next President and the MM keeps pumping that statement in anticipation of the crash. They are now pushing the narrative **'the stock market has predicted the outcome of the election of the President since 1984'.** Keep your eyes and ears open out there!!

Gates recently publicly stated he wants to see the medical community vaccinated first, then the blacks. Perfect. I've also seen that our military is at the top of the list to receive the vaccine when available.

Gates and co. could literally euthanize every doctor, nurse, medical, fire and police personnel in our country, and our military. Someone has to stop him and the only ones who can are you and me, friend.

If I was a black man and awake to the NWO agenda I would take particular exception to Gates' wishes. Gates is a eugenicist, aligned with the thinking of the founder of Planned Parenthood, Margaret Sanger. Sanger is a *documented* eugenicist-racist. I'm telling my Black brothers and sisters right now to BEWARE of this agenda to vaccinate them among the first!!!! BLM should be protesting against Planned Parenthood and not burning down their neighborhoods!!!

Unfortunately, I'm expecting major events going forward. Every time I turn out one of these reports our situation has deteriorated further, not gotten better. I expect this to continue.

The current protests/demonstrations/riots are only a taste of what's to come as groups are added to the mix. Soon the patriots who are tired of wearing masks/being quarantined/watching the country go down in financial and societal flames will begin to demonstrate and I expect this group to clash hard with the BLM/Antifa crowd.

Don't worry, once the food begins to run short both groups will be put upon even footing against 'the man'. I also expect antivax protests once the covid-19 vaccine becomes near or available, and who knows what else will come up to get people pissed off...this year is only just past half over!!

Recently Jeffrey Epstein's girlfriend/cohort Ghislaine Maxwell was arrested and currently in custody....when will she 'kill' herself? The global pedo-network is coming unraveled. So many have come forward about it... crazy times. Going to get crazier...

Now they're saying there is a coin shortage!! All the more reason to just submit to 100% using your debit/credit cards so they can 100% track everything. This is like a bad movie playing out in slow motion, in **REAL LIFE!!!**

What's happening, unfortunately, is that what I predicted in my first book, the Culling of Man, is coming true.

Is our government really that inept that it can't put enough coins into circulation to facilitate transfer of goods and services? You know, those business transactions that its taxes depend on for survival?

People and businesses were starting to shun cash because it's 'dirty' and might have covid-19 on it when this first started. Now I regularly see signs that they don't take cash anymore. Throw in a coin shortage and heck, might as well just give up on cash!! We are being both pulled and shoved into 1984!!

Now the truth be told, the covid-19 death rate **WITHOUT** a vaccine is lower than the annual flu deaths **WITH** a vaccine.

They've never been able to come up with a coronavirus (common cold) vaccine before in history. Why will they be able to do it now and so quickly?

Because all the world's a stage and they arguably already have the 'vaccine' all ready to go.

I expect it to be complete with delayed-timing 'side effects' that won't show up until everyone has been vaccinated and it's too late to stop the side effects.

And ol' Billy Gates and co. will not have a shred of liability about it thanks to the Vaccine Injury Act of 1986!!

Perfect.

I intend on sticking around a long time WITHOUT a vaccine, I've got a third book to get out. The following pages will most certainly be a chapter in the upcoming book…the proponents of the Great Plan are currently setting the stage for Civil War II.

Civil War II

"Violence is immoral because it profits from hatred. It destroys the unity and makes the brotherhood between people impossible"

"Nonviolence means not only avoiding not only external physical violence but also internal violence of spirit. You not only refuse to shoot a man, but you refuse to hate him"

"We must forever conduct our struggle on the high plane of dignity and discipline. We must not allow our creative process to degenerate into physical violence"

-Martin Luther King Jr., various quotes about how important it is to gather, march and protest peacefully in order to be taken seriously, in order to have true and durable change.

****

The following passage comes from my first book, "Rise of the New World Order: The Culling of Man", full pages 282-285:

****

"I see in the near future a crisis approaching that unnerves me and causes me to tremble for the safety of my country. As a result of the war, corporations have been enthroned and an era of corruption in high places will follow, and the money power of the country will endeavor to prolong its reign by working upon the prejudices of the people until all wealth is aggregated in a few hands, and the Republic is destroyed. I feel at this moment more anxiety for the safety of my country than ever before, even in the midst of war."

-Abraham Lincoln

"The division of the United States into federations of equal force was decided long before the Civil War by the high financial powers of Europe. These bankers were afraid that the United States, if they remained in one

block and as one nation, would attain economic and financial independence, which would upset their financial domination over the world. The voice of the Rothschilds prevailed... Therefore they sent their emissaries into the field to exploit the question of slavery and to open an abyss between the two sections of the Union."

- German chancellor Otto von Bismarck

A strategic opportunity dropped into the Illuminati's lap when social divisions over slavery began to develop as the United States grew more powerful. They fanned the sparks of this issue knowing that they could take control of America through debt if they could divide the North and the South ideologically and then prod both sides into a long and costly civil war--which they would of course be funding from both sides.

"It is not to be doubted, I know with absolute certainty, that the separation of the United States into two federations of equal powers had been decided upon well in advance of the Civil War by the top financial power of Europe."

- Otto von Bismarck

Four years before the war in 1857, the Rothschilds decided their Paris bank would support the South, represented by Sen. John Slidell, a Rothschild agent, from Louisiana; while the British branch would support the North, represented by August Belmont (Schoenberg), another Rothschild "employee", from New York.

The plan was to bankroll, at very high interest rates, the huge war debts that were anticipated, using that debt to blackmail both sides into accepting an Illuminati-owned central bank. Propaganda by their minions pushed the issue of slavery to the public forefront, but the actual purpose behind the war without question was to drive both sides to accept a privately-owned central bank---just like we have today.

As in pre-Revolution France, Illuminati agitators were sent to work in the North and the South at all levels of government and throughout society to exploit the divisive issues threatening the nation. In the years following our independence, a close business relationship had developed between the cotton growing aristocracy in the South and the cotton manufacturers in England. The Illuminati decided that this business connection was the United States Achilles Heel.

Their carefully sown and nurtured propaganda developed into open rebellion and resulted in the secession of South Carolina on December 29, 1860. Within weeks another six states joined the conspiracy against the Union and broke away to form the Confederate States of America, with Jefferson Davis as President.

Even members of then-President Buchanan's Cabinet conspired to destroy the Union by damaging the public credit and working to bankrupt the nation. Buchanan claimed to deplore secession but took no steps to check it, even when a U.S. ship was fired upon by South Carolina shore batteries.

Shortly thereafter Abraham Lincoln became President, being inaugurated on March 4, 1861. Lincoln immediately ordered a blockade on Southern ports, to cut off supplies that were pouring in from Europe. The "official" date for the start of the Civil War is given as April 12, 1861, when Union-controlled Fort Sumter in South Carolina was bombarded by the Confederates, but it obviously began at a much earlier date.

This quote from earlier in the book is worth repeating:

"The money powers prey upon the nation in times of peace and conspire against it in times of adversity. It is more despotic than a monarchy, more insolent than autocracy, and more selfish than bureaucracy. It denounces as public enemies all who question its methods or throw light upon its crimes. I have two great enemies, the Southern Army in front of me and the bankers in the rear. Of the two, the one at my rear is my greatest foe."
-Abraham Lincoln

Lincoln said he feared the money powers (Illuminati) more than the Confederacy, and with good reason as you now know.

After the war, realizing the Union's real enemy was Rothschild and the Illuminati gang, President Lincoln, emphasizing the Constitution, made it crystal clear to Congress that:

"The privilege of creating and issuing money is... the supreme prerogative of government!"

Abraham Lincoln, although never taught in our public schools, fought a legendary battle with the Rothschild bankers after the beginning of the Civil War over who was going to finance the war from the Union side. Lincoln ultimately followed the Constitution and issued money through the federal government---allowing him the financial power to win the war and keep the country intact. As you now know, this is the real reason he was assassinated. If he would have lived, the greenbacks he issued would have become the norm for the United States, and the Great Plan would have been derailed.

For this and other acts of patriotism, Lincoln was shot down in cold blood by Illuminati agent and alleged 33rd degree Freemason John Wilkes Booth on April 14, 1865, just five days after Lee surrendered to Grant at Appomattox Court House, Virginia.

Booth's grand-daughter, Izola Forrester, states in her 1937 book "This One Mad Act" that Lincoln's assassin had been in close contact with mysterious Europeans prior to the slaying and had made at least one trip to Europe. Following the killing, Booth was allegedly whisked away to safety by members of the Freemasonic Knights of the Golden Circle. According to Forrester, Booth lived for many years following his disappearance, safely hidden away in Europe by the Illuminati.

3Truth to be told of the Civil War, and again, this is suppressed history you are not supposed to know about, the real cause of the Civil War had little-to-nothing to do with freeing the slaves, and everything to do with fighting off the Illuminati and saving the Union, and it is a FACT that Lincoln made the following two quotes:

"I have no purpose to introduce political and social equality between the white and black races. There is a physical difference between the two, which, in my judgment, will probably forever forbid their living together upon the footing of perfect equality; and inasmuch as it becomes a necessity that there must be a difference, I ... am in favor of the race to which I belong having the superior position."

And:

"My paramount object in this struggle is to save the Union, and is not either to save or to destroy slavery. If I could save the Union without freeing any slave, I would do it; and if I could save it by freeing all the slaves, I would do it; and if I could do it by freeing some and leaving others alone, I would also do that.."

624,511 American citizens died in the Civil War, and 475,881 soldiers were wounded because of the Luciferians attempting to further the Great Plan.

"The death of Lincoln was a disaster for Christendom. There was no man in the United States great enough to wear his boots and the bankers went anew to grab the riches. I fear that foreign bankers with their craftiness and tortuous tricks will entirely control the exuberant riches of America and use it to systematically corrupt modern civilization. They will not hesitate to plunge the whole of Christendom into wars and chaos in order that the earth should become their inheritance."

- German chancellor Otto von Bismarck

Unfortunately, the proponents of the Great Plan were just warming up for something much bigger.....the first truly World War.

****

(End of *"Rise of the New World Order: The Culling of Man"* section)

****

The same people who caused the first Civil War to happen are the EXACT same ones fomenting Civil War II.

You've been warned.

Ratcheting up the Great Plan

"By this plan we shall direct all mankind. In this manner, and by the simplest means, we shall set in motion and in flames. The occupations must be allotted and contrived, that we may in secret, influence all political transactions ... I have considered everything and so prepared it, that if the Order should this day go to ruin, I shall in a year re-establish it more brilliant than ever."

-Adam Weishaupt, mastermind of the Illuminati

Remember from my first book, The Culling of Man, the original goals of the Bavarian Illuminati?

These are the people who rule the planet today mind you!!!

1. Abolition of the Monarchy and all ordered government.
2. Abolition of private property.
3. Abolition of inheritance.
4. Abolition of patriotism.
5. Abolition of the family/morality and communal education for children.
6. Abolition of all religion.

Let's run through this list, one by one, really quickly and see where we are today, shall we?

They got rid of virtually all the Kings and Queens running Europe from back in their day. The ones that are left are fully vested with the pedo-Satanists and are 100% on board with the Great Plan/New World Order.

Abolition of private property? That sounds exactly like something called socialism to me...uh oh.

No wonder they have been promoting socialism in the public-school system so much recently. More Millennials are socialist than not if you talk to them, and Generation Z will be worse. The number of Millennials who wanted to see Bernie Sanders as President was disturbing to say the least.

They just don't understand how socialism really works. It fails. Every time. WITHOUT FAIL it fails. Miserably.

These are the exact same people who will be taking the reigns of power someday and it will end badly for us all.

They know their future looks bleak and they bought into the socialism pipe dream hook, line and sinker.

Abolition of inheritance? This goes hand-in-hand with abolition of private property. They want everything you own to be turned over to the state when you die instead of being able to amass wealth, which would be a threat to their power.

Don't know if you've checked the 'inheritance tax' lately, aka the Federal Estate Tax, but if you leave your kids more than about $12 million the graduated tax increases quickly up to 40% of the money.

Now, I wouldn't be complaining to inherit that kind of money (!) but if the feds are going to take nearly half of it as it passes hands to the next generation you can see how that money power can be beaten down quite handily by the inheritance tax, generation-by-generation.

If you amass a fortune worth $100 billion, like say... **Bill Gates**, and want to leave it to your kids? They will get only about $60 billion. $40 billion goes into the Federal Government's black hole of debt.

This is the main reason for the tax-free foundations the elite started setting up at the beginning of the 20ᵗʰ Century, again all in my first book.

This is exactly why Gates now has the 'Bill and Melinda Gates Foundation', to shield their wealth, not to help humanity but to HARM humanity and protect the interests of the pedo-Satanists running the planet.

"Abolition of Patriotism"....here we go *rolls eyes and sighs*...

This is a HUGELY important topic to a guy like me who bleeds red, white and blue!!

I'm proud to be an American, but the NWOwned Mainstream Media is beating it into their followers that the USA is an evil, racist country and we need to destroy it and start over as socialists!!! OVER MY DEAD BODY!!!!

This is an attack on the people who ARE proud of what our country has accomplished as one, giant melting pot of people from all walks of life banding together to make us into the greatest nation the world has ever seen.

Unfortunately, we are also the most immoral, corrupt and war-mongering thanks to the guidance of the proponents of the Great Plan and a blank check from the Federal Reserve starting in 1913.

This ATTACK on US, my fellow Americans of all shades, colors, creeds, religions, etc. has been in the works for a long time but ramped up significantly after 9/11...

After 9/11, the Military Industrial Complex, aka the proponents of the Great Plan, had all their Neocon puppets in place when the false flag we know as 9/11 went off.

"We", meaning the USA as a whole--citizens, business and government-- invaded a handful of largely black/brown peoples' countries, *largely Muslim populated*, and murdering millions over a manufactured lie.

The USA is now nearly universally hated worldwide for this and other empire-building exercises like the Gulf War, and since most people in the world associate the United States with naïve/entitled white people and white Christian men in particular, you can see how easy it is to work up the 'people of color' against the white man in America today.

Europe is in an interesting spot also with all the 'refugees' that were brought in for what is coming. Can't say anything about any of this though because if you talk about racism and AREN'T a card-carrying leftist-activist then you are a RACIST!!!! That's the pot calling the kettle black!!!

And now this kneeling business when it comes time to play our National Anthem before we sit down to watch the weekly bread-and-circus show the elites are still putting on after thousands of years?

Rome burned to the ground because everyone was intentionally distracted while the country went down in flames?? By the time the people realized it, their Empire had been dissolved. It was way too late…kind of like today.

Unreal.

If you want to disrespect our flag and our country that's your business, but I'm not going to support YOU doing it and neither are millions of other patriotic Americans.

We are not going to or watching your circus-sports anymore, full of entitled, spoiled brats of ALL colors with no concept of how blessed they are to have the talents they do and to make the kind of money they get.

Nowhere else in the WORLD could they get this kind of money, fame and attention and then they turn around and sh!t all over our flag and country on primetime teevee, broadcast globally by the NWOwned media, making us look the fools all over the world. Unreal.

"Abolition of the family, elimination of societal morals and state-indoctrination for the children".

I don't need to tell you of the divorce rate, I think it's around 50%. My childhood was severely negatively impacted by the divorce of my parents as are millions of others, and that's the plan.

The Baby Boomers, living through the excess of the 1970s and 80s felt that having a good time was more important than toughing things out and trying to make a marriage work like the old days. At least that was my situation in 1986 when my parents divorced, sending me at 16 years old careening headlong into alcohol and drugs to rebel against everything. I'm working on a separate book about that actually, how it's a miracle that I'm alive today after all the craziness I've been through in my life. I guess I had to be kept alive to turn these books, right? Right.

The state-indoctrination leapt into full-swing with the advent of 'Common Core', which I covered in the last update book. The result is that we have two generations of vaccine-damaged, fluoridated, medicated and confused kids who think that their only future rests with socialism. Ugh.

Lastly, 'Abolition of religion', or at least all of the different religions in favor of the one world religion, the worship (again) of King Nimrod/the Antichrist.

Hmmm....seems that the local governments have largely shut down all churches in the name of 'public safety' but you can still go to the store and buy liquor, weed, junk food, etc. but ohhhhhh-nooooooo it's not safe to go to church for an hour once a week.

There have even been parishioners and clergy ARRESTED and put in JAIL, where there is now plenty of room because the gooberment lackies let out tons of prisoners to make room for the religious and patriotic!!!

Ok, enough of this, I'm starting to get riled!!!

Anti-fascist…but pro-socialist…?

'Antifa' is more an ideology than an organization because anyone can say they are part of Antifa.

Even though they are aligned with BLM/Black Lives Matter, they are very different.

They say they are anti-fascist, but the bulk of them are staunch socialists which is just as bad as fascism. Both ways have always been controlled by the proponents of the NWO, and have always ended badly for humanity without exception.

Since Antifa isn't an organization with a charter, business license, etc., they are ripe to juice up with buckets of cash from the likes of George Soros and company.

I've seen the ads from Craigslist all over the country looking to hire agitators at $200 per day and they would cover any attorney fees if you got arrested.

They are routinely caught bussing these paid rioters in to cities after collecting them up from around the countryside because there aren't enough people in the cities who will riot/cause mayhem/distraction to turn attention away from what's going on in DC, the plannedemic, the economy, etc.

This isn't a 'movement' at all but a well-financed terror operation controlled by the globalists and supported/promoted by their mainstream media.

The people who participate as 'Antifa' aren't truly anti-fascist, they are socialist-anarchist extremists.

The Great Plan has been mapped out years ahead of what is happening today. These agitators were planned long ago to provide a distraction from what is happening in the world as things start to unravel.

There is a massive pedophile ring coming unraveled right now and it has to do with Hillary Clinton's and others' emails put out by Wikileaks, of which the body of evidence is collectively called "Pizzagate".

Also, Jeffrey Epstein/Ghislaine Maxwell and a huge host of Hollywood celebrities, business moguls and government elites whose names are all over Epstein's documented flight logs aboard the 'Lolita Express' are starting to feel the heat of public scrutiny.

Antifa will be there as agitators _against_ the coming riots involving the patriots who call BS on this plannedemic, the anti-vaxxers who will be against mandatory vaccinations, and anyone else calling out the NWO agenda to destroy us all going forward.

By starting "riots" at what would otherwise be peaceful demonstrations, the cops will by default declare a riot and disperse everyone, effectively nullifying the real patriotic Americans' rights to peacefully assemble and protest in large numbers under the First Amendment. See how this is going to work?

They are establishing now a very vocal and physically aggressive minority, and when I say minority, I mean just a few thousand people out of 330 million, and most are paid at that.

Since they've aligned themselves with BLM, we are getting exactly what Rev. King was railing against back in the 60s: Riots. Looting. Burning. Vandalism. Assaults on the innocent.

Globalist George Soros founded and bankrolled his 'Open Society Foundations' to the tune of $38 billion. OSF is a huge bankroller of both Antifa and BLM. Anything and everything to take down the US.

"The main obstacle to a stable and just world order, is the United States"
-George Soros, his book 'The Age of Fallibility', 2006

Bottom line: Antifa are largely paid agitators to distract us by occupying media time-space, further terrorize an already 'pandemic'-weary population and help push us to the brink of Civil War...II.

Nothing says justice for George Floyd like white Millennials dressed in black pushing the black community to burn and loot their own neighborhoods to push 'racial justice'...

Black Lives Matter!

Many people in our society, mostly 'white' leftists, view the slogan 'Black Lives Matter' as a call for help, a call to action.

These same people promote BLM on their social-media profiles, carry BLM signs at protests and shout slogans, and make financial donations to an organization they probably know nothing about other than what they are spoon-fed by the NWOwned media.

Like I just said, nothing says justice for George Floyd like a bunch of out-of-state, white Antifa protestors who were paid cash by George Soros to destroy black communities while screaming at the top of their lungs that 'black lives matter'...unbelievable.

Unfortunately, when white-guilt-ravaged-Joe-average-liberal-white-guy-or-girl donates to this tax-deductible (!) organization they are unintentionally helping to bankroll the destruction of the USA. They do this by helping fund pre-planned manufactured divisions between each other in order to help facilitate the destruction of our country.

The Great Plan is working masterfully well I must say...

"Myself and Alicia (Garza) in particular are trained organizers. We are trained Marxists."

-BLM founder/leader Patrisse Cullors in a 2015 interview, speaking about co-founder Alicia Garza

The 'Black Lives Matter' movement basically began as a social network hashtag, #blacklivesmatter, in July 2013 after the acquittal of George Zimmerman in the murder of Trayvon Martin.

BLM gained strength in numbers and notoriety in 2014 following the demonstrations over the deaths of Michael Brown in Ferguson, Missouri, and Eric Garner in New York City.

The movement really gained steam earlier this year when on May 25, 2020, a short video clip went viral of a black man being pinned to the ground by the neck by a white police officer in Minneapolis. He subsequently died and BLM was thrust back into the spotlight thanks to dozens of riots nationwide and calls to defund/eliminate the police.

Let's stop right here and see what all the fuss about racism lately is *allegedly* about...

BLM claims that American society is patently racist from top to bottom and that cops in particular have it in for black men, killing them wantonly. Virtually an epidemic of racist killings by police against black men.

Truth be told, the deadliest enemy of the black man is other black men in their community, and it has to do with selling drugs and 'turf wars' over who gets to sell drugs in any given area.

More white men than black are shot and killed every year by police, but no matter what color the deceased are, the common denominator in these shootings is drug abuse, and drug abuse is rampant in the inner city where most of the nation's black community resides.

You will NEVER have peace in the black community until the drugs have been removed from the equation, which the entrenched BLACK drug dealers have no intention of letting happen. So, we have what we have today unless the fascists at BLM can fix it "with enough donations to their cause"...oof.

Corporate America has jumped on the media-mandated, PC-bandwagon with donations to the Marxist terrorists at BLM from Microsoft, Apple, Google, Facebook, Walmart, Target, etc., including matching donations from their employees to BLM.

All of the above multi-national corporations are pro-globalist by nature and therefore by default are anti-USA/nationalism and pro-NWO/globalism.

This donation activity also insinuates that these companies are left-leaning, since they are factually backing a Marxist movement and the fact that the Great Plan for the global enslavement of mankind and one world government is a leftist, socialist agenda governed by the unseen elites at the top with their puppet politicians...just like always.

Let's talk about George Floyd now. The entire incident, not just the short clip blasted all over the media of the white officer with his knee on the neck of Floyd on the ground screaming that he couldn't breathe.

The body cam footage of Officer Thomas Laine was released on 8/11/20 and I watched the whole thing, start to finish. The original incident happened on 5/25/20...2.5 months earlier. That's all the public has seen until the body cam footage release a few days ago.

I watched the video and it starts with the cops heading into the store where George Floyd had tried to pass a counterfeit $20 bill. They go back outside and Floyd is sitting inside a minivan in the driver's seat about 100 feet from the store. The cops approach and make contact with him, getting him to open the van door and finally, eventually come out, where he is put in cuffs and under arrest. The cops were surprisingly patient with Floyd who continuously defied their orders to get out of the van. They get him out and cuff him.

Then it starts to get crazy. Even before Floyd was under arrest and sitting in the driver's seat of the minivan he was crying and saying he couldn't breathe. I've done enough hardcore drugs like meth and coke to know how they feel and how they can influence you in any given situation. He knew he was in BIG trouble with the law and he was high as hell on either fentanyl or meth/crank, or both and was starting to freak out.

Now I've seen closeup screen captions of Floyd's mouth when he was sitting in the driver's seat of the van. He has a small, white thing in his mouth. If this was fentanyl, it's no wonder he died that day as he was holding enough fentanyl in his mouth to kill 100+ people!!

Not only this, it was shown that he had advanced heart disease and was on the verge of a heart attack and dying as it was before this incident ever took place.

The fact is that George Floyd was a convicted violent felon on parole and he knew he was going back to prison for violating parole.

He might even have been going back for good, I don't know and now we'll never know, but he did some pretty heinous stuff before this incident ever even took place including holding a gun to a pregnant woman's belly while his friends robbed her home!!

The FACT that the four officers who arrested him were Asian, Latino, Black and white shows that this incident had NOTHING to do with racist cops but a drugged out, probation-violating felon…a violent career criminal.

As I'm watching the video he is freaking out because he knows he's going back to prison for passing counterfeit money. He is completely combative and won't get into the police cruiser to go down to the station because he knows he is screwed, he's high and he's resisting 4 officers at once!

The video is sad because it's like he knows he's going to die, but not because of anything the officers did other than try to arrest him.

He's saying *'I can't breathe. I love you mama'* over and over. It was his will that he would rather die than go back to jail. Not being able to breathe is a side-effect of a fentanyl overdose. He was probably overdosing as he was sitting in the van seat with a mouthful of fentanyl.

Overall, it looked like a pretty standard arrest of a drugged-out, violent man, and the cops were even more polite and even calm than I would have expected for the situation.

One of the cops said "I think he's passing out"…Floyd DYING right there probably wasn't on their minds as that **rarely** happens.

It certainly does appear that the cop on his neck didn't help Floyd's situation and may have been what ended his life, but bottom line his knee wouldn't have been there if Floyd had cooperated to start with, and not resisted violently…it took 3 cops to hold him down on the ground.

These poor cops have to deal with drugged-out violent criminals day in and day out. They don't know what the guy is going to do. If he's got a gun, a knife, a used needle full of heroin and AIDS.

Again, I would concur that Chauvin, the cop who had his knee on his neck, should have better assessed the situation when it appeared that Floyd had passed out/died. I can see justifying an excessive use of force charge, but murder? And all four cops charged with murder? I don't agree with that.

The entire situation would not have happened if Floyd had cooperated, bottom line.

The whole video is just a sad state of affairs of the inner cities of the United States caused by drugs. Drugs that have been introduced by the CIA into our society since the 1960s. Selling drugs on one hand to fund their black ops and slowing but surely helping to kill the USA on the other through the denigration of life and society thanks to the aftermath of drug addiction and abuse. The CIA was well known to be flooding 'Contra Coke' into the inner cities in the 1980s to cause addiction and a demand for more coke for black ops cash.

At the point in the video they load Floyd into the ambulance it appears they think he passed out and is not dead.

George Floyd did not die because he was black. He died because he was high on more than one majorly dangerous drug, meth and fentanyl, and was panicked because he KNEW he was going back to prison so he resisted arrest because of his crazed state of mind, to the point of death.

Let's briefly look at Floyd's life to see what kind of trouble he was in prior to this particular incident, and see where his life went awry.

George Perry Floyd Jr. was born in North Carolina on October 14, 1973 and died on May 25, 2020 at the age of 46.

Floyd moved early on and grew up in Houston. As a teen, George Floyd was a star football and basketball player for Jake Yates High School. He graduated in 1993. He then played basketball for two years at a Florida community college. After that, in 1995, he spent a year at Texas A&M

University before returning to his mother's home in Houston to seek jobs in construction and security.

Everything, to me, seemed to be going along good for George. He graduated high school. He attended college. He had no trouble with the law and was seeking gainful employment in his younger adult years.

Looking at his arrest record/timeline it seems he took up drugs after moving back to Houston, and it was all downhill from there.

In 1997 it appears he was arrested for the first time in his life for selling drugs. Probably to support his new drug habit I'm guessing.

1998, arrested for theft. Again, probably to support his blossoming drug habit.

1998 again, arrested for theft...again.

And this goes on and on until he has been arrested and been in and out of jail a total of nine times through 2007 for everything from drugs to aggravated robbery with a deadly weapon.

Floyd basically wore out his welcome in Houston, so when he was paroled he moved to Minneapolis in 2014.

It appears from the public record that he sort of had his life back on track, after moving away from Houston and old habits. At least he was working instead of selling drugs apparently.

But old habits die hard and it was found by the autopsy that he had both meth and fentanyl in his system, both highly addictive. And dangerous I might add, not only for the person who ingests these calibers of hard drugs but for the people around them.

Looking back when I used to do those kinds of drugs in my 20s, those drugs like meth/cocaine/opiates literally allow your demons to come out and take over your entire being whether you believe in God or not, and have a huge influence on your mental, spiritual, and physical actions.

I feel bad for George Floyd, I honestly do. I KNOW what he was going through. I myself was addicted to these kinds of drugs and beat them all finally.

George Floyd's death has little to nothing to do with racism and everything to do with drugs. Drugs are the real problem between the cops and the blacks in the inner city. Any racism that abounds is a side-effect of the inner-city drug culture where drug dealers are viewed as cool and upstanding members of the community tossing a $500 wad in the collection plate at church on Sunday.

Addiction needs money to buy drugs, which causes people to sell drugs, rob and steal, and prostitute themselves to get drugs to feed their addictions.

This illicit demand creates a market and since there are no rules for this illegal market it's every man and woman for themselves, unless they form gangs to control a certain area of the market they control and protect with gun fire.

The cops are then forced to try and maintain law and order in the middle of literally hundreds of 'mini wars' going off in the bigger cities over who controls the drug territory. That's it. That's the root of this problem with cops and black men. Drugs. Not racism, drugs.

So this guy George Floyd had his life derailed at an early age from a promising young black athlete to a career criminal because of his drug addictions.

This is the man that BLM and Antifa are holding up as a prime example of how a harmless, unarmed black man was victimized by the cops???

I feel bad for Floyd getting pulled into the black hole of drug abuse but he is no role model at all. He's exactly the example of how NOT to turn out in life.

Let me know the next time the cops kill a black doctor, nurse, lawyer or even a black cop. If the white cops are out to get the black men of America surely any cop who is black must be quaking in his boots from his co-workers, right? WRONG.

And BLM/Antifa trying to use this particular situation as the spark to bring 'racial justice' for black and brown people? These people are absolutely insane. They are doing the black community WRONG and the patriotic blacks in the US needs to stand up and tell these Marxist agitators that they do NOT represent the black community and to STOP trying to come across like they do!

I surely don't hear the Asians complaining about anything. Don't all Asians have brown skin?? Aren't they "people of color" too? Am I missing something here??

Surely if the big, bad white man hated and discriminated against black and brown people he would have kept the Asians down too, right? WTF? The Asians are passing the whites in virtually all scholastic testing these days!!

And how about the other, past upstanding members of the "black community" that had highly-publicized run-ins with the cops?

You know, the ones that the media used to goad the blacks into burning and looting their own communities time and time again.

Rodney King ring a bell? Almost a billion dollars in damage, nearly all of it in the Los Angeles black community. If you look into it, King's situation mirrors Floyd's exactly: Addicted to drugs and would do anything to get them.

When Rodney King was arrested, he was high as a kite on PCP, a drug I've never done and never even considered doing as it has about the worst reputation of all illicit drugs because of what it can turn you into: a literal demon in the flesh with superhuman energy and strength.

There have been a handful of incidents between the founding of BLM and the George Floyd incident that BLM has blown up into a media sensation for no other reason than to further their own Marxist agenda, which is also the NWO agenda so they aren't going away.

If BLM **_really_** cared about black lives, they would be protesting at the front door of their local Planned Parenthood...

"Colored people are like human weeds and are to be exterminated."
-Documented eugenicist Margaret Sanger, founder of Planned Parenthood, spewing her vile, racist rhetoric

It seems that if there were ever a cause to bring attention to over whether or not black lives mattered to the black community and not just a handful of donation-collecting Marxist-socialists, it would be education about abortion and where and how it came to be so destructive to the black community. It seems black America has been targeted from the get-go by Planned Parenthood for termination if you look into it.

Black women constitute only about 13% of the female population in the United States, but they undergo approximately 1/3 of the abortions performed in the US annually.

As a result, nearly 2,000 black people are aborted every single day in the United States!! This is state-sanctioned mass murder in my book. This is a trap set by the NWO that is tough to fix. Because of drugs. Again.

The average black, inner-city kid grows up without a father, listening to music that glorifies violence, drugs and womanizing, lives in a community where murder is a regular occurrence and the drug dealers run the streets. Surely the police aren't this kid's biggest problem, it's drugs and the side effects of drugs, one of which is friction with the cops who have to try to enforce the law of the land.

The best thing a black family can do for their kids is to move the out of the city. Break the cycle. Have faith that you can do this because you can! You live in the United States of America and you can still pick up and move wherever you want to in this country....just do it.

Nobody I know is on board with this BLM crap. Not my black, brown or white friends...NONE.

People of ALL COLORS are sick of the lawlessness, the riots, the attacks on honest businesses owned by people of all walks of life, attacks on white people/history in general, the threats and demands.

The only thing BLM has accomplished is to live up to the ghetto stereotypes they ought to be working on changing instead of reinforcing by looting and burning in the name of Marxism....in the name of the Great Plan.

Wholesale Media Brainwashing

"The most brilliant propagandist technique will yield no success unless one fundamental principle is borne in mind constantly: It must confine itself to a few points and repeat them over and over."
-Adolf Hitler's Minister of Propaganda, Dr. Joseph Goebbels

It is through the NWOwned mainstream media where BLM and Antifa get their power, using a propaganda campaign cooked up long before George Floyd came along. A massive distraction to keep people's attention off the facts surrounding the plannedemic.

A relatively small, boisterous, aggressive group of radical like-minded people who are for tearing down the current system and eliminating everything that goes with it. They want society to be absorbed by the socialist state they will create, which will then enforce their Marxist agenda.

Now take that tiny minority of people who actually believe in their cause and add a few thousand or more paid agitators making $200 a day to run the streets causing chaos instead of finding a job.

Who knows how many of those 'protestors' are there because they actually believe in their cause as opposed to hired rioters? We'll probably never know.

And now these pseudo-terrorist organizations are **_corporate-backed_** for the destruction of the USA by Microsoft, Google, Apple, etc. This needs to be broadcast from the rooftops that they are helping to destroy us all!

Where were all the black activists who say the Confederate flag is racist for the last 150+ years since the Civil war began? Nary a peep about it even during the 1960s when ALL GRIEVANCES WERE AIRED and if it wasn't brought up then it shouldn't be an issue today. But people are being TOLD it's an issue today, which is triggering them to action.

Social Justice Warriors were prodded by the NWO-owned-and-controlled media with a single false flag. That one white kid who was shown on the media holding a Confederate flag and shot up that black church a few years ago. They showed that image of him holding that flag over and over and over until the SJWs were whipped up into a frenzy. I watched it with disgust it was so obvious.

Same with Trump! He wasn't a "racist" until he decided to run against the Democrats and the media sold it to the sheep that Trump was a racist. He's anything but in my opinion based on the FACTS.

They sell him as a racist because he wants to enforce our borders? Even going so far as to build a wall? Undocumented people aren't flooding into our country from our northern border with Canada, but that is happening at our southern border with Mexico and it's got to stop. Mexico has a wall at their southern border to protect their country from illegal immigration from Guatemala, why shouldn't we???

It is funny to me to hear some people talk about misappropriating 'people of color's' culture.

I'm sorry, were you speaking to me in English...? You know, the *whitest language on the planet*???

Hey! STOP USING <u>MY</u> LANGUAGE! The ENGLISH language you use? That's 100% created by whites for whites to communicate with other whites about white-people stuff and I am HIGHLY OFFENDED. YOU'RE MISAPPROPRIATING MY CULTURE!!! THAT'S MY LANGUAGE!!! MINE MINE MINE MINE MINE MINE!!!!

Just kidding of course. But that's how stupid some people sound these days.

Look, you live in the United States of frikken America, the most diverse country on the planet. You don't get to come to me and say I can't do this or that because you're going to be offended. This is America, Jack! We SHARE our cultures here. We ARE the great melting pot we've always been referred to.

Well the Great Plan can't tolerate people getting along together because they might get together and hang them all so the media is now nonstop pushing the NWO/Illuminati/ agenda, which is now the agenda of the left in case you haven't noticed.

The left's line-item-agenda reads like something out of Bizzaroworld where everything is backwards: Climate change is caused by mankind so we need draconian laws, taxes and bigger government to fix it. I agree pollution is bad, but the facts show that the solar cycles are what influences our weather, not mankind. The real facts of this are in my first book.

Illegal immigration is good, borders are bad and racist.

Masks, vaccines, etc. are good for your health.

Police are bad, we can work things out ourselves.

Oh, and EVERYTHING is racist except the extreme left's positions so don't offer up an opinion different from what 'they' are seeking to establish as the new norm.

Read Goebbels quote again at the top. If you turn on NPR radio, CNN, MSNBC, or the like it's 3 main topics day in and day out now for months: the USA is racist and white people are evil, the pandemic will kill us all if we don't conform to what we're told, and it's all Trump's fault. That's it. Over and over and over beaten into the heads of their listeners, who take that agenda and start implementing it bit by bit through their daily decisions.

The mainstream media is slowly but surely radicalizing the left into socialism ala Hitler's playbook. Remember, the Nazis were socialists!!!

"Nazi" is literally shorthand for National **Socialist** German Workers Party!!!

None of the Democratic Presidential candidates spoke out about the riots but supported them! Look what happened in Seattle, the city council told the cops to STAND DOWN AND LET THE PROTESTORS TAKE OVER THE POLICE PRECINCT!!!

We are heading down a dark road with martial law and the end of the USA at the end of it.

The media is seeking to tear the country right in half and it's the paid actors on teevee who are spoon-feeding it to the sheep. And if that news guy or girl doesn't want to say what they are told they are down the road and will never work again because they just want talking heads spewing propaganda not actual journalists up there on the nightly news.

Real journalists don't make seven or eight-figure salaries, ACTORS do.

I'll leave you with one more quote from Goebbels, he's telling us quite a bit of truth here:

"Every age that has historical status is governed by <u>aristocracies</u>. Aristocracy with the meaning - the best are ruling. Peoples do never govern themselves. <u>That lunacy was concocted by liberalism.</u> Behind its "people's sovereignty" the <u>slyest cheaters are hiding, who don't want to be recognized."</u>
- Joseph Goebbels

Conclusion

So. As a man of 'no color', can I be offended for just one minute here about the current state of our society?

I am **PISSED OFF** at how our country is being divided up with everyone against everyone when we should be uniting against the problem we've had with each other since around 2,200 BC: King Nimrod's Great Plan.

Now we've got black vs. white.

We got masked vs. no maskers.

We got left vs. right.

We got pro-manmade-climate change vs. It's the Sun/natural cycle.

We got pro-life vs. pro-choice

I get sick to my stomach watching what's going on. A patriotic guy like me watching our country go down in flames from everything going on. This is not going to end well, not at all.

There's room for everyone here to get along, but the Great Plan is seeking to move the agenda forward and needs everyone at odds with everyone else. They need everyone bickering so we are too busy, wore out or burned out to give a hoot that they are jerking the rug out from under us as we argue amongst ourselves!

Our country is taking on water and sinking fast because everyone is at each other's throats!!

For all the "rampant and institutional" racism that the leftist-Marxists are clamoring has been going on in the past right to the present day 2020, there sure are a **LOT** of black people all over the media in sports, movies, music, television, etc....they must not have gotten the memo that whitey doesn't allow them to experience the American Dream of actually making it and being able to afford to live comfortably, have a secure retirement, etc.

You know, those things that virtually NOBODY is able to achieve anymore?

It takes a two-income household just to make the bills these days and I'm one of those households, but I still love my country to DEATH.

To me, judging by the population ratio in the USA, blacks seem OVER-represented in sports/multimedia. And you know what? I DON'T HAVE A PROBLEM WITH THAT AT ALL.

I **WANT** to know about black people, their culture, their family life, etc.... that's what any good American would want! To better know their neighbors so we can have each other's backs.

Blacks are uniquely "black" way beyond skin color, just as whites, Hispanics, Asians, etc. be it music, food, culture or whatever.

Being black should be viewed as a positive and not a detriment as the mainstream media is blaring out. They are right now on the mainstream media telling young black kids that their future in the USA is diminished because of the color of their skin and that's a blatant LIE.

Blacks are FULLY VESTED in seeing that the USA stands strong. Blacks are not only over-represented in the media but also in our MILITARY and that says to me that blacks have a significant stake in patriotism to the USA. Nearly 1/3 of the active duty females are black!

The media is trying to alienate the black community away from being patriotic Americans through all this kneeling during the National Anthem crap. Hopefully the silent black majority will speak up someday and quash this or it's just another nail in the coffin for all of us in the USA.

Blacks that have been here for generations are as American as baseball, apple pie and Chevrolet for god sakes. Blacks are an integral part of what we are as a whole, as the united citizens of all walks of life that make up the USA.

Black Americans have contributed immensely to the POPULAR view of the United States worldwide, our cultural side as a nation, instead of the largely-"white" war-mongering US government/NWO side murdering millions of brown and black people worldwide in the name of 'democracy', which is code for 'New World Order' in case you didn't know.

Now listen up, because here is the truth that the mainstream media WILL NOT put out there: White people didn't start slavery in the United States but white people ended it!! My ancestors and countrymen of ALL COLORS died for the cause of freeing the black slaves in the United States during the FIRST Civil War.

Not only this, if the United States and the patriotic "white" man in particular hadn't stood up en masse against Hitler and Hitler would have won???

There probably be any black or brown people alive on the planet today to complain about "whitey"...YOU'RE WELCOME BLM!!!!

Look. Mankind of **ALL RACES** have been conquering and enslaving their fellow man since we were put here about 6,000 years ago.

Before the white man ever set foot on the North American continent the Native American tribes waged war against each other, took each other's land and looted, enslaved, murdered and raped the losing tribe...FACT!

There are FACTUALLY active slave traders RIGHT THIS SECOND in the Middle East buying and selling black and brown people!!

Where is BLM on this???

Where are the corporate titans voicing concerns about this? Crickets.

Where was Antifa and BLM when the US was bombing the "people of color" in the Middle East back to the Stone age after 9/11? Millions killed and tens of millions more wounded over a manufactured LIE. I guess they didn't matter...?

Oh, that's right, most of the people protesting today WEREN'T EVEN ALIVE WHEN 9/11 WENT OFF AND THE ONES THAT WERE ALIVE WERE PROBABLY STILL CRAPPING THEIR DIAPERS ALL THE WAY TO AGE TEN!!

These protestors are largely Millennials and Gen Z. All vaccine-injured, fluoridated, medicated and indoctrinated into the New World Order view of the world that socialism and a one world government are their only hope.

Well let me tell the Millennials and Gen Z something (my kids are Gen Z btw) about living life in the United States since I was born in 1970, since you weren't here to know.

I'm a **highly-observant** person in case you can't tell, and my long-term memory is crazy-good. I have taken in everything I've observed and hear very intensely over my 50 years. I was always a listener instead of a talker, always observing and learning about life around me.

I don't want to sound like a crusty, old codger, because I'm not...but these youngsters these days have no idea how things were not all that long ago and how good we had it here in the USA in terms of race relations.

For the most part, everyone got along great after the 60s, I'm talking blacks, whites, EVERYONE.

The 1970s were an unbelievably fun time to be alive.

Let's start with the music! Blacks and whites REGULARLY AND WITHOUT ISSUE hung out together at concerts, night clubs, discos, etc. There were none of this crap these days where 10 guys jump one guy and beat him gang-style. That ridiculousness wouldn't fly in the 70s. People of all colors would have jumped in and stopped that type of behavior. Now it is condoned. Videoed. Shown on social media for the amusement of others.

The music being put out by the black community in the US was insanely good when I was a kid...and timeless. Good music will always sound good and be remembered. Earth, Wind and Fire. The Jackson Five. Stevie Wonder. And on and on and on.

In the 70's it was super-trendy, fashionable and COOL to feature blacks in all forms of tv and movies, etc.

The #1 show of the 70s was 'All in the Family', a show that poked fun at the small minority of bigots in the US. It was so good it spun off 2 or 3 'black' shows which were themselves huge hits.

I used to love to watch the Jeffersons on the first go-round in the 70s and then on reruns in the 80s.

I remember coming home from school in 1978 and watching 'What's Happening' with Dwayne, Rerun and Roger! And of course, Shirley at the dishing out one-liners!

That was some good, clean, funny BLACK humor without all the bathroom jokes and sexual perversion in everything these days. Sanford and Son. Good Times. And those shows were right alongside Dukes of Hazzard on a Thursday night or whatever WITH NO PROBLEM FROM A SINGLE SOUL IN THE UNITED STATES AT THE TIME YOU WHINY, PUSSIFIED BRAINWASHED BRATS!!!!

Obviously, any tirade I'm on is not directed at my awake brothers and sisters who are just coming into their teens through 30s. I think you understand however where I'm going with this: WE are in a bad spot for our country, at it is **YOUR GENERATIONS WHO WILL SUFFER THE MOST GOING FORWARD.**

YOU'VE GOT TO GET ACTIVE!!!!

My kids are Gen Z and I'll fight for their future to the end, to MY end.

Back on track: In a nutshell, everything was going great in the 70s for all the races, creeds, colors, etc. At least according to the media and society at large for the time and to this day. Prove me wrong!

Then the 80s came and everything got nice and cozy between everyone as we all settled into the 80s for a **CRAZY** ride together, the 1980s really were over the top on all fronts...but everyone was still getting along GREAT.

"We all know that people are the same where ever you go
There is good and bad in everyone
We learn to live, when we learn to give
Each other what we need to survive, together alive
Ebony and ivory live together in perfect harmony
Side by side on my piano keyboard, oh Lord why don't we?"

-From the #1 hit song 'Ebony and Ivory' by Paul McCartney and Stevie Wonder, 1982

Remember Crocket and Tubbs? OK forget I brought that up, but all through the 70s and 80s there was nothing but positive interactions between blacks and whites throughout the mainstream media. This is because this is the truth of how people felt coming out of the 1960s...everyone was ready to be friends and neighbors finally so that's what was reinforced through the media. The media is now being used to steer that sentiment in the opposite direction to divide us once again and people need to wake up.

Most people in the United States don't know or care but 2020 was the 35th anniversary of Live Aid.

What is "Live Aid" you might be wondering? It was a concert held in 1985 simultaneously in both London and Philadelphia at the same time and broadcast globally with the intent of raising money to feed the starving people of the African country of Ethiopia, who were undergoing a brutal famine at the time.

The elites could have saved them with the flick of a pen!!! But nooOOoo....it was up to the largely "white" people to step up and help out the blacks who are STILL IN AFRICA AND WERE NEVER SLAVES BUT "WE" HELPED THEM ANYWAYS!! The citizens and performers from the United States and Great Britain stepped up and helped out their fellow mankind.

The organizer, concert performers and fans in attendance of these two shows were 95% or more WHITE.

But the mainstream media told me that whites are racist and hate blacks.... what happened here? That's right, whitey didn't get the memo that the whites aren't supposed to be nice to the blacks, especially in other countries.

And how about the blacks in sports throughout the 70s and 80s who were my heroes as a kid?

Earl Campbell, a BLACK guy, to this day is my all-time favorite football player. When he burst onto the scene in 1978 as a rookie with the now-defunct Houston Oilers, he made that big of an impression on me as he was so exciting to watch when he was handed the football. His thighs were as big as tree trunks and he would literally just run over people! You never knew what was going to happen, which of his plays would end up on a highlight reel, always on the edge of my seat. I was enamored with him lol. I even had his jersey as a kid when all my friends had Bradshaw, Largent or Zorn lol. It's been a few months but I still go to YouTube and watch the old videos of him doing his thing

Then heading into the 1990s, things were still just fine between all the races in America.

It was after 9/11 that things changed, everything changed because we were entering a new phase of the Great Plan.

I grew up on the construction sites in Washington state right out of the gate, I've been pulling nails out of 2x4s since I could hold a hammer. Right out of high school I started my career in construction and have worked on jobsites right to this day.

Let me tell you for a FACT. On a construction site it doesn't matter what color you were, you have to prove your worth **as an individual** because on a construction site ain't no one else wants to pick up your slack or carry your dead weight when we're being paid the same amount of money so it's largely sink or swim.

I swam just fine and pinnacled with me eventually running multi-cultural, multi-million-dollar jobsites. I do my own thing now running my handyman business, but I used to be a big roller on the jobsite. I had a hundred guys or more at once working on my jobs. We'd build about 50 condos at one time/phase.

Mexicans. Koreans. Russians. Blacks. Whites. You name it. These are the people who literally built America in the construction trades since we all started building it together in 1776.

As they all worked my site, we became friends seeing each other day in and day out, sometime for years at a time. I used to thank them for doing me right and even threw big parties for the workers at the end of every job. Everyone came too as we all were friends, we all knew each other's worth as individual humans because we'd be working around each other all day and enjoyed being around like-minded, hard-working people...of all races.

There is a certain respect on a jobsite among the workers of all ethnic backgrounds that I sure wish would bleed over to mainstream society, it would be a change like you wouldn't believe.

Come to think of it, that WILL happen when the Master Carpenter Himself, Yahushua (Jesus) comes back to wad up the Great Plan and the pedo-Satanists and chuck 'em in the jobsite dumpster!

I've got one more quote from Martin Luther King Jr. here, and considering that the main reason there is friction between blacks and whites today is not because there actually is, *but because the media is telling us there is and people are buying into it and the media keeps stoking this fire.*

"We must learn to live together as <u>brothers</u> or we will perish together as <u>fools</u>"
- Martin Luther King Jr.

As I was finalizing this report it was announced that Kamala Harris is the NWO's pick to be the next ~~Vice President~~ President of the United States.

I firmly believe that Trump will win but the election will be flipped to Biden. He'll bow out not long after being sworn in...if not before the election!!

I can't even believe he'll make it that long honestly. Have you heard him speak lately? He's completely all over the map with his speech, something is clearly wrong with him. That still leaves the door open for Hillary as VP!! I would 'lol' that but our fate would be sealed and nothing funny about that.

Also of significance is that since my last report the Pentagon released "formerly classified" UFO footage. Predictive program much???

Remember the quote from my first book from President Ronald Reagan addressing the UN General Assembly about how all nations and peoples of the world would unite against an alien threat? Project Blue Beam....look it up.

This covid-19 vaccine-situation that is coming is not good. After it comes out, if you don't have it **you will be denied entry to any schools, colleges, universities, hospitals, doctors offices, Emergency Rooms, ambulance service, etc.**

If you are getting ANY aid from the government like unemployment, food stamps, welfare, etc. you will be REQUIRED to get the vaccine if you want to stay on the gooberment teet. You watch how they will turn the thumbscrews on those dependent on the government to survive, especially with what's coming.

If you come down with a serious illness like cancer and absolutely have to go to the doctor and are like me who will refuse the vaccine to the bitter end, you have my sympathy. At that point I would be seeking out Bill Gates and co. in person for some payback for humanity!!!

Basically, if you refuse the coming vaccine you are going 'off grid' while living in the middle of the grid!!! No medical help. Limited shopping opportunity. Etc. This is coming people!!

The mandatory masks are to prepare us for the Mark of the Beast by denying people right now to do business for not wearing a mask/conforming to the "rules".

Soon it will be, no contact tracer app, no service, ...then it will be no RFID implant, no service. Because if it is not inside your body, you could loan out your phone or have a burner phone or whatever and then be running around contaminating the rest of the population over a virus not even as dangerous as the flu!! The NWO can't have that now! *rolls eyes*

Revelation says the mark will be in the right hand or forehead... remember Bill Gates' RFID tattoos from the last update??? Have you had your temperature taken in public lately? THEY SCAN IT ON YOUR FOREHEAD!! They want to familiarize you with this simple action of reading information coming from your forehead.

They. Want. To. Track. YOU...!!!

If the masks are soooo effective why didn't they mandate them from the start since Fauci and co. supposedly know soooo much about viruses and vaccines. Heads should have rolled already!!!

If the 6-foot rule works, why the need for masks? If the masks work, why the need for 6-feet of separation? If both are working then why a lockdown? This is not for our safety; it is conditioning to obey the state, including a mandatory vaccine.

You watch, they are going to meld this 'social distancing' crap right into Agenda 2030.

This will mean only 25% capacity for movie theatres/concerts/assemblies/etc. and prices will be proportionately higher...300-400% price increases coming on these kinds of events or they won't be worth putting on. This is going to get ugly people.

I see the Nasdaq just hit a record high! The higher it goes the harder it will fall. During Trump's "normal' economy, which was flying high, I could see those valuations, but we are barely even seeing and feeling the effects of what is coming.

There are big time businesses folding up right this second. It will all catch up to the markets just in time to jolt them for the election.

I'm guessing about September for the big crash right before the election so they can pin that on Trump as the main excuse he "lost" the election. Oh, and the pandemic he caused. Oh, and he was the cause of all the racism too. The jury is still out for me on Trump, whether he is actually for us or in on the Great Plan, but the poor guy has been under attack by the media from day one, unlike Obama who had nothing but praise from the leftist lapdog media during his tenure.

The covid-19 numbers are all over the map since my last report.

Confusion is a staple of a big false flag and this is the biggest of all. There was just a huge scandal in Florida that got swept right under the mainstream media carpet: cases of covid-19 were overreported by 90%!!! This is happening all over....completely crazy and blatantly wrong numbers.

The proponents of the New World Order are terrorizing our seniors and robbing our kids of their future inside a gutted United States. If we don't rally, we're done.

I can't stress enough how important it is to have my first book in paper that can't be touched electronically by a 'worm' that could be released by the proponents of the Great Plan to electronically ERASE everything they don't want you to know about...that which they will legislate to be ILLEGAL to pass around. 1984 is now.

The people that run the planet arguably have the power to 'erase' the entire internet digital record, leaving only paper-written or printed files left. How could they do this besides a 'worm'? Only a couple dozen nuclear devices set off 250 miles above the planet would do just that...a massive EMP strike globally to erase digitally everything that wasn't deep underground in the private and military survival bases.

They could literally sterilize the entire Earth of virtually all electronic records, except the ones they possessed, so the proponents of the Great Plan can start fresh with the _New_ World Order.

1,000 apologies to those like myself (!) who **prefer** to read a paper copy of anything over staring into a pulsating monitor or phone. I don't have the means to put these update reports into paper form unfortunately, so just print it up and read it like I would lol. Then you can pass it on to your neighbor that way!!

I print these reports...and my books...over and over myself to read on paper. It's a HUGE difference in terms of taking it in. I read the digital versions of everything I put out and when I think it's good enough, I then

PRINT it up and WOW what a difference it is to read…and edit. And edit. And edit.

Thanks for all your support over the years and I HIGHLY encourage anyone that wants to throw in with me, for you to start writing books on all the various sub-topics to do with the New World Order and publish them yourselves! It's VERY EASY to do this on Amazon's Kindle and we need to blitz our peeps to shake 'em up, wake 'em up.

Writing this update was an emotional roller coaster for me, I hope it wasn't too much for you. If you ever have time to pray for me, I'd sure appreciate it my friend!! I won't go into detail here but I've had bad situation after bad situation unfold for me this entire year, surely things that are making me wonder if I'm being targeted by the proponents of the NWO.

Yet again, until next time my brother and sister sentinels //////

May YAH watch over you and yours and guide you as safely as possible through the rest of 2020, we've still got a long way to go.

YAH bless all.

-Sentinel Jeff Hays

RISE OF THE NEW WORLD ORDER: BOOK SERIES UPDATE AND URGENT STATUS REPORT VOL. 4

NOVEMBER 20, 2020

<u>Intro</u>

Hey friend!

As I'm putting this update through it's final edit, we're in the chaotic days after the 2020 election.

All those mail-in ballots I talked about in previous updates are being used to do exactly what I said was going to happen: the NWO is trying to steal this election and put their chosen puppets into place.

All things considered it appears that Trump really was on the side against the NWO, or at least played the part of it very well. He surely does seem to be on the side of the awake, patriotic Americans who were against the politics-as-usual and the globalists being in control of the USA going forward, aka the proponents of the New World Order.

Remember, the NWO/Republican Establishment didn't want Trump...at all.

Republican stalwarts like John McCain, Mitt Romney, George W. Bush, etc. all were against Trump and still are...except McCain obviously, but his widow is supposed to be on the Biden transition team coming into the White House!

Trump didn't rise up in their circles and was therefore not beholden to the same entities as the D.C. left and right Establishment players. Trump was truly an outsider when he showed up looking to be President in 2015.

And then he won in 2016 despite it all and was a bull in the NWO's globalist china shop, taking us out of the TPP, the Paris Climate Accord, didn't start any new wars, etc.

Trump made policy decisions with a *nationalist* outlook, which is good for the citizens of the United States because that means that he put us first, and the rest of the world second.

This resulted in having one of the best economies EVER **<u>with record high Black and Latino employment</u>**---everybody was working and doing great.

That is not how the globalists want things for the USA so they pulled the trigger on the plannedemic to excuse getting Trump out and the NWO back in control.

Now that they have their puppets Biden and Harris ready to take the helm it's full steam ahead, and Biden has already promised to implement the following on record, multiple times, once sworn into office...NWO coming in **HOT**:

- nationwide mask mandate, probably with stiff fines for non-compliance. People will be snitching on each other left and right over this. Welcome to Nazi Germany circa 2021.

- complete shutdown of the economy in order to 'stop the spread' of COVID-19. This will basically finish off what economy is left that was able to find a way to make it so far. Say goodbye to your favorite restaurant.

- mandatory vaccine in the name of stopping this proven-non-deadly virus, at least until the 'mutation' happens, which I'm still expecting before this is all over.

- making addressing 'climate change' the number one priority and to begin building our economy around this new NWO-backed religion. That's right, I said religion because it is a belief in something you cannot see, complete with rules and regulations---how you should and WILL live your life according to this incoming tyrannical government...or else.

- extreme gun control and possible forced buybacks

They are still sorting out this election business, and we might not know for weeks or even MONTHS who is going to be President as it is hashed out in the courts.

If I was Trump, I'd be arresting Biden right now from the treasure trove of evidence that has surfaced lately via his son Hunter Biden's recovered laptop.

Trump called it the 'laptop from hell' and he is right. There is evidence on there that Joe Biden is beholden to China, and his son Hunter was compromised by them via filming him engaging in sex with underage Chinese girls, among other wholesome activities like smoking crack on camera.

People like you and me who see what's going on behind the political scene are now in a bad position because we are at the mercy of the uneducated masses who helped install Biden/the NWO, even though I believe Trump legitimately won the election by a landslide.

I have my doubts that Trump will be able to overcome the power of the NWO with regards to this election fraud but if he does, he could very well use the laptop evidence to put away Biden and a host of others it sounds like. Trump and his people seem pretty confident he is going to win in court.

Just like Hillary said in the Wikileaks emails, if one goes down, they will all go down and I just don't see that happening, they are collectively vastly too powerful and entrenched in the world power structure.

We're talking the real Illuminati here, the ones who own the Federal Reserve, started the UN, etc..... the Rothschild/Rockefeller contingency.

Remember, people like George Soros and Bill Gates WORK for the Rockefellers, who are worth trillions.

There are probably enough Masons and Jesuits in positions of judicial power up and down the ladder to trip Trump up if required. With 6 of 9 sitting Supreme Court Judges being Catholic (Jesuit) and Biden being Catholic (Jesuit) watch out! The number is actually 7 if you count Gorsuch, who was raised Catholic by Jesuits but reportedly attends an Episcopalian church now, so who knows.

The one thing Trump could do that would do more damage than anything in the WORLD would be for him to hold up my first book at a press conference and tell everyone to read it!!

But that would never happen and it would probably be the end of me jabbing at the NWO.

As much as I want to stop them, the Bible says I won't be able to, and these things must come to pass in order for Yahushua/Jesus to make His return and smite the NWO for good.

I don't know if there will come a point in time when writing these reports and ultimately my books will matter anymore to anyone, but as long as we still have free speech of some sort and aren't under martial law restrictions, I will keep working to put my take out there on what's going on, time-willing, as I'm able.

With what's going on this year it's like the wheels just came off at the start of the year and we've been witnessing a slow-motion car wreck that just keeps going...and going...and going. You never know what the day will hold in 2020, and we're not done yet.

I actually had some remodel work drop in since the last update so I've been busy work-working to pay my bills, but I still made time to work on this fourth update as we're ALL running out of time to learn as much as possible about the New World Order, what has happened, and what's going to happen soon.

I am going to keep this update/piecemeal chapter-train rolling so I can turn the third book of this series in a timely manner. 1000 apologies again for getting out of the game in 2017 to relocate my family to what I deemed a safer place knowing what was coming, what we're in now. I'm finally settled back in and now I'm back writing again....lookout!

Some of the contents of this update are going to be a chapter in the third book of my 'Rise of the New World Order' series of books.

This particular chapter will be a *sequel* to chapter 7/Methods of Madness in Book 1: Rise of the New World Order: The Culling of Man.

I'm giving you *'Methods of Madness II'*....YIKES!!

"Methods of Madness II" is basically a hit list of various consumer products that the globalist corporations are churning out for not only profit but to help facilitate the destruction of the United States in particular by destroying our health.

A sick society is a weak society. They need us weak so we will fall....right into the waiting hands of the global government, aka the United Nations. If people knew the facts of what is in this chapter it would radically change their consumer habits, it has mine and probably will yours also if you are unaware of what we're going to go over.

And of course, **I HIGHLY recommend getting my first book in paper form before this type of information is stricken from the internet and only the paper records will stand to tell the truth of our situation.**

Facebook sent out notices in August that on October 1 they would begin heavy censorship and they are following through.... "**Facebook** will remove or restrict access to any content on the platform that can bring legal or regulatory risks for the company all over the globe..."

Not only that, even CONGRESS passed a resolution condemning the existence of conspiracy theories on social media/the internet! Search for H.Res.1154!!

The proponents of the NWO are turning up the heat with 1984 coming in hot, renamed 2021 now.

We'll do what we can, while we can, to wake people up, one final trumpeting of the truth to awaken the Called.

Remember from my first book, it took knowing the facts of our seemingly awful situation politically and religiously to 'wake me up' to the fact that we have been living under King Nimrod's Babylonian Mystery Religion for the last 4,200 years.

So, I've got something here for you to ponder...that I believe to be true to our situation, and it's both good and bad at the same time.

Again, I'm going to put this disclaimer right out here in the beginning of the report: before we go over the following information from my second book, **"Rise of the New World Order 2: The Awakening"** and everything else I put to paper, you should view what I'm saying as my *opinion* based on facts researched and concluded by me personally for my own sake. I'm just putting what I believe into books to pass on to others.

You may look at the facts and come to a completely different conclusion and that's why we're here: To come to our own conclusions personally after taking in everything we can factually on any number of topics.

I felt it was too early where we were as a society to talk about the subject of the End Times. I released my second book in 2015 and edited out this particular section in 2016 as that book was heavy enough thinking without throwing in my End Times outlook.

Given the dire state of today's world, I feel the time is right to put it back out there for research and comment by my readers, clergy and the public at large.

This information will certainly be included in Book 3 of the 'Rise of the New World Order' series, which I'm hoping to release early-to-mid 2021. I'm staying on track thanks to the interest in these updates so thanks a ton for throwing in with me if you're reading this! Knowing I have backup helps to keep me motivated.

The following is excerpted from the original version of "Rise of the New World Order 2: The Awakening", released in 2015, pages 113-115. For your reference, the "Book of Jasher" is referenced in the Bible as being legitimate, which is why I used it for my own calculations of an End Timetable:

.... The Book of Jasher is also highly interesting in that there is substantial information about King Nimrod, **including a scene directly between Abraham and Nimrod of literally Biblical proportions!**

King Nimrod, the founder of the Babylonian Mystery Religion and the Antichrist himself vs. God's chosen human representative whose descendent Jesus would be the very one to quash Nimrod's quest for immortality. I'll leave all those quotes for another book, or for you to discover, but there is one more item from Jasher that jumped out at me as I was going through it.

The Book of Jasher actually gives a timeline of the Biblical events, starting from the creation of mankind to the death of Joshua, denoting time in 'AM', which stands for 'Anno Mundi', which itself means 'Year of the World'.

By taking the date of the death of Moses, which is listed as 2,488 AM in the Book of Jasher, and comparing it to when Biblical historians say he died, we are able to work backward and forward from this date until we come up with a total of about 6,000 years.

It is my opinion that from the time mankind was placed here in the form we know him as today, to the culmination of the End Times, would be right about 6,000 years. This is because numerology is not only important to the occultists running the world, but because God was the one who made those numbers important to begin with.

It is my *opinion* that in this situation God is treating 1,000 years as a day in His world, and on the seventh day, which would be the seventh millennium of our existence, this will be the beginning of the Millennial Kingdom. This is exactly **why** it is called the Millennial Kingdom; it is virtually a **Sabbath Millennium** of global peace, love and worship of Jesus.

By taking the date the Book of Jasher says Moses died, 2,488, which is counting forward remember, and adding it to the approximate date theological historians say Moses would have died, which ranges from 1,450 to 1,270 B.C., you would get a range of 3,758 to 3,938 years from the time mankind appeared to 0 B.C. Add today's year of 2015 (2,015) and you would get a range of 5,773 to 5,953 of approximate years lapsed since the Millennial Kingdom clock was set into motion. **This would leave 47 to 227 (or so)** more years to go until the **Millennial Kingdom, which equates to the return of Jesus.**

The prophesized one world government would have to come immediately before this, **which is in existence today at the United Nations**. We are only one global calamity from causing the nations to fully succumb to the United Nations as the true one world government of the End Times.

This global calamity will arguably be the global financial collapse that is coming. That's my front-runner in the big picture of things. It might not come this year or next, but it will come and it is being prepared for on many fronts, with the most visible being the ever-growing global police state.

While researching this theory that Jesus' return could be imminent, I came across the following verses to help corroborate my hypothesis:

"But do not ignore this one ****fact,*** ***** beloved, that with the Lord one day is like a thousand years· and a thousand years like one day."**
-2 Peter 3:8

And also:

"Lord, you have been our refuge through all generations. Before the mountains were born, the earth and the world brought forth, from eternity to eternity you are God. You turn humanity back into dust, saying, "Return, you children of Adam!" A thousand years in your eyes are merely a day gone by...."
-Psalm 90:1-4

Sir Isaac Newton was also doing some calculations on this, and he stated that the Millennial Kingdom would not begin any sooner than the year 2060. The dates above I'm giving range from the year 2062 to 2242.

I personally give much more credence to a date closer to 2060 as opposed to 2242, and when I saw his date virtually match my closest date, I had an epiphany we are truly near to His coming. He obviously arrived at his conclusion the same way I did, but not finding this out nor the Biblical verses above until *after* I had considered the way I could make an approximation only makes this estimation all the more plausible.

"It may end later, but I see no reason for its ending sooner. This I mention not to assert when the time of the end shall be, but to put a stop to the rash conjectures of fanciful men who are frequently predicting the time of the end, and by doing so bring the sacred prophesies into discredit as often as their predictions fail."
–Sir Isaac Newton (1643-1727) giving the date of 2060 as the earliest possible start of the Millennial Kingdom

Everything seems to be coming together exactly as prophesized, so don't despair over this for sure. It should only be reinforcing the faith among the brethren in Jesus Christ, that we have made the correct life choice in surrendering ourselves fully to Him while we had the chance. I thank Jesus every day without fail for saving me.

I'm going to build on the above scenario I have laid out, taking into consideration what I've learned since putting it out there in 2015.

Let's take the above date of roughly 2060, and work backwards according to the biblically-derived amount of time in a generation, 70 years.

We are using this number because of the importance of the timing of the End with regards to the parable of the budding fig tree in Matthew, Mark and Luke's books, and the relationship of the rebirth/replanting of the Nation of Israel/fig tree.

70 from 2060 is 1990. Israel was reformed in 1948, but was not officially recognized by the Vatican/Unholy Roman Empire until 1993. King Nimrod/the Antichrist/first Sun God is the god of the Pope/Vatican/Catholic Church, you know this from my first two books.

Roman Catholicism is just the old Roman Empire's Sun God worship with a Christian veneer, complete with the same ancient Babylonian holidays.

King Nimrod is the original Sun god from which all after are dedicated to, this is why Christmas/Easter/Lent/etc. are based on Nimrod's Babylonian Mystery Religion of Nimrod/Semiramis/Tammuz.

What happened in 1993, is that I believe the Antichrist himself set in motion the events that will lead to the End and his return to once again rule the world, briefly, by himself recognizing, through his mouthpiece the Vatican, that Israel was re-established. 1993. Nimrod sees from his spiritual prison what is happening on Earth and directs his people to do his bidding. He could see his people had finally pioneered the DNA technology needed to bring him back from the grave to rule the world once again as prophesied exactly in Revelation.

Only 3 years after setting the clock in motion in 1993, it is made public that scientists have successfully cloned their first animal using a sample of DNA, Dolly the Sheep....remember that?

Also keep in mind that black ops labs are 20 years or more ahead of what is put into the public arena. The Illuminati's DNA scientists and laboratories are literally the best that money can buy and far ahead of anything being performed at universities or the corporate world.

Add a generation to the 'confirmation' of Israel, you get 2063, within 3 years of the 2060 date by Newton, and within 1 year of my date 2062, of the possible, and I feel probable, beginning of the Millennial Kingdom.

"Now learn the parable from the fig tree: when its branch has already become tender and puts forth its leaves, you know that summer is near; so, you too, when you see all these things, recognize that He is near, right at the door. Truly I say to you, this generation will not pass away until all these things take place. Heaven and earth will pass away, but My words will not pass away."
-Words of Yahushua, Matthew 24:32-35

This same scenario is also outlined in Mark 13:28-31, and Luke 21:29-33.

Yahushua is saying when the fig tree, which was planted in 1948, starts to bud and put forth its leaves, that's when the clock is set in motion at approximately 70 years.

The budding leaves represent the means to bring Nimrod back from the dead, today's incredible DNA technology. This is the sign that Nimrod is going to make his return according to the Great Plan.

It is my *opinion* that Nimrod was physically brought back into this world on 9/11/01, that was literally his re-birthday. There is much more to this than I have time or space to get into here about that, but I will expand fully in book 3 of my series. **_I do believe the Antichrist is alive today and is about 20 years old._**

If the Millennial Kingdom begins in 2062, take 7 years off that for the Tribulation = 2055. Nimrod would be in his mid-50s taking the world into the Tribulation....he would rule 10-20 years before that I'm guesstimating, making him mid-30s to mid-40s when he took over the world around 2035 to 2045. Don't sell him short by being able to take over the world by 35, he is the Antichrist after all.

This is probably where they got the date and the program from the United Nations called Agenda 2030. They want everything in place for him to step right into the leadership position. The Green Religion has to be fully in place by 2030 and they are pushing it hard right now. Climate Change will be the excuse to subdue mankind for the Beast.

Now, let me tell you why he is called 'the beast' in the Bible. It's because Nimrod was the first Nephilim post-Flood. He's part man, part angel and I believe that angel to be Azazel/Satan/Kronos/Saturn. I have all of the evidence to show this in an upcoming book, but for now you just need to know that the DNA sample that they took Nimrod's sample from to reanimate him is literally *Nephilim* DNA.

This is partly why the End is so near I believe. The Illuminati cannot be allowed to possess DNA technology AND Nephilim/divine DNA to play with. Big no-no there and that's what caused the 'Flood' event to happen to kill off all of the chimera abominations that were created in the days of Noah.

We're in the days of Noah RIGHT THIS SECOND!

"For the coming of the Son of Man will be just like the days of Noah. For as in those days before the flood they were eating and drinking, marrying and giving in marriage, until the day that Noah entered the ark, and they did not understand until the flood came and took them all away; so will the coming of the Son of Man be."
-Matthew 24:37-39

Since Nimrod is a Nephilim they would have had to have probably engineered out of his DNA the 'giant gene' because he was probably 12-feet tall or taller.....and he was BLACK!!

Nimrod was a *Hamite*, which would make him African.

Since Nimrod was and will be again part-angel, he will have demigod-like intellectual capacity and power since he's got 'angel DNA'. He could even have literal super powers like mind control or who knows but this would help explain how he is able to hypnotize the masses into following him like a pied piper straight to hell.

Now it's also possible that the Illuminati DNA engineers were able to change Nimrod's appearance to be more of an average of what everyone looks like on the planet because he has to appeal to everyone, but I can say that I highly doubt the Antichrist would look like a white dude... like the classic image of "Jesus" that was foisted upon Christianity by the Vatican.

That image everyone is familiar with as 'Jesus' worldwide is factually of the son of Pope Alexander VI, Cesare Borgia!!!

That's the entire purpose of the Second Commandment not to have any graven images, statues, or anything representing the Divine...because most people don't question anything!! Millions of people are praying to a picture of the son of a Pope who represents the Antichrist on Earth!!

Absolute and complete blasphemy. Off the chart deception. Same as the holidays.

We are heading into the most exciting, terrifying times humanity will have ever experienced. The Days of Noah. Those kinds of crazy events that have happened this year are here to stay.

If you are awake, saved and ~~following~~ studying everything I've talked about up to this point, this quote from Revelation 17:8 should make complete sense to you now, knowing just how decadent, unrepentant, depraved, backwards, naïve, mean and just callous a lot of the population is today:

"The beast, which you saw, once was, now is not, and will come up out of the Abyss and go to his destruction. The inhabitants of the Earth whose names have not been written in the Book of Life from the creation of the world will be astonished when they see the beast, because he once was, now is not, and yet will come."

What this quote is saying, is that the beast/Nimrod/the Antichrist once existed here on Earth in physical/spiritual form, that his physical form was not around during the writing of the book Revelation, but he will be back someday in the future to rule the world again.

Nimrod died and his spirit went to the Abyss (a spiritual jail) where he is the king of Satan's demonic army (Revelation 9:11). The people on Earth whose names were NOT written in the Book of Life, aka the people willfully following along with the NWO agenda including being microchipped/mark of the Beast, will be told that this upcoming glorious new global leader IS THE ACTUAL BIBLICAL ANTICHRIST and they will still follow him knowing they will be damned for eternity.

I'm guessing this whole Nimrod-Antichrist situation will be fully out in the open in 10-20 years from now, it has to be. Nimrod WANTS to take credit for Christmas being a factual dedication to him. He WANTS people to know that Easter is really a ritual to his mother-wife, Queen Semiramis/Ishtar/Eastre/Isis and nothing to do with Yahushua/Jesus. He wants maximum blasphemy and he will get it.

You, the person reading this now, are on the cutting edge of what is going to come out in the next few years and decades. The truth of Nimrod and his Babylonian Mystery Religion is still largely unknown, even to most clergy-types.... Not. A. Clue.

The elites/Illuminati/Deep State/ruling pedo-Satanists know all about it, it has been their game plan for the last 4,200 years.

And I'm sure they know I know about it. In fact, I would be very surprised if they HAVEN'T read my first two books just to see exactly how close I got to the absolute truth of what is really going on in ~~our~~ Satan's world.

They know the truth.

Methods of Madness II

One single component of what we're going to go over here usually won't do you in.

It is a combination of many components all at once, over time, that overwhelms the body's natural defenses, and cancer in particular sets in at your weakest link.

The following sections are all further dangers I found after 'waking up' to the NWO in 2007 and publishing my first book in 2013.

These are the kinds of issues that should be taught in school instead of virtually non-existent "social justice" issues that were nowhere to be found for thousands of years and are suddenly everywhere... according to some.

Well, I found out about these "real life" issues through my continued research into all things we're not told about in the corporate-controlled Mainstream Media because they want us sick and run down in order for us to fall at the feet of the incoming tyrannical global government.

These hazards I'm listing are now always on my radar, to make sure my kids in particular are either not coming into contact with these hazmats, or if they do, to minimize the danger as much as possible through understanding the mechanics of the danger.

By understanding the truth about the globalist multinational corporations putting profits before humanity, you will understand what we are up against when it comes to the many different COVID-19 vaccines coming down the pipe.

Their lobbyists were at work years before the plannedemic…at least since 1986 when they got Congress to give them blanket-immunity from lawsuits arising from side-effects of the vaccines they knew they would be cranking out as technology increased.

With minimal and absolutely no long-term safety testing, a rushed vaccine with no legal liability (Vaccine Act of 1986) will be a gold mine for any number of globalist corporations, and there are literally HUNDREDS of COVID-19 vaccines in clinical trials right now.

Lucky us.

Acrylamide

After I woke up in 2007 and then researched, wrote and published my first book about the New World Order and their ancient Great Plan in 2013, I had a guy track me down to thank me for what I had done in putting my first book out there.

He was sort of awake like I had been, but needed the info in my book to fully tear down the facade of what was REALLY going on in order to fully awaken.

He himself had written a book to tell his own story after almost dying from getting his mercury fillings extracted a few years earlier. He had to learn how to heal his body using detoxes, cleanses, eating certain things and NOT certain things, etc.

Through the course of his research for his recovery he discovered the dangers of ingesting acrylamides. I had never heard of this substance before but immediately alarm bells starting going off as I read on and found out that acrylamide is a toxic substance we come into contact with every day without warning! That is, except in California where they actually DO warn you about it!

I've got a funny story from my childhood about this acrylamide business...

When I was growing up we'd visit my grandparents a couple of times a year, and invariably, every time we were there, we would have a tableside discussion with my grandpa about 'eat your crust, that's the best part'....so I did, even though I didn't like the taste of the 'burned' part of the bread.

My grandparents went through the Great Depression and stretched every resource they had and could, right up until their passing. Not eating the crust would be wasting food, which was wasting money, which was a big no-no in their household. Fast forward forty years and I now go out of my way NOT to eat the crust on a sandwich. In fact, first thing I do is tear the crust off and throw it away.

And why is that you're probably wondering?

Because the "burned" part of the bread, the dark crust, contains acrylamide. When bread, potatoes, or some other popular foods are cooked past a certain point, the surface starts to chemically-react and turns into a plastic-like substance called acrylamide. That's the crust on your bread and also the face of the bread you just toasted, so now it's got acrylamide on all 6 surfaces!

That's also all sides of a French fry, that 'skin' is acrylamide... which is technically burned potato....now a cancer-causing toxic plastic when ingested.

Acrylamide has been in our presence since the dawn of mankind, fire and then bread obviously, but this *fact* wasn't even known to mankind until Swedish scientists first discovered it in certain foods in 2002.

It took them that long to figure this out??? Doubtful. More like suppressed.

At least California, for all the screwy crap that has gone on there, showed a sign of sanity by passing Proposition 65 that actually warns of the danger of ingesting the bread because of the acrylamide content.

Proposition 65 went into law in California in November of 1986, and acrylamide was finally added to the warning list in February of 2011. If you are in California your bread, French fries and other products should have Prop 65 label with an explicit warning about acrylamide.

A few Summers ago, I was out of town and I went to buy a loaf of bread at the local supermarket in Washington State where I've lived all my life. I'm pretty perceptive being awake and all, and looked over the whole loaf, damage to the outer wrapper, fat/fiber content, etc. and noticed an odd warning on it, from the State of California from all places. It had the California Proposition 65 label on it warning the consumer of the danger of acrylamide in the bread from the crust and more so after toasting it and making even more 'crust'.

I was shocked, surprised and then delighted that there was actually some action on this largely unknown danger because I knew about the danger of acrylamide at the time...and I knew that fact would eventually end up in one of my books to warn my readers, so here you go!

It was the first and only time I've seen that warning in person, so the bread must have been shipped up here from California.

Acrylamide is not only a naturally-occurring substance in cooked food but is also a man-made chemical used mainly in certain industrial processes, such as in making paper, dyes, and plastics, and in treating drinking water and wastewater.

There is also acrylamide in some consumer products, such as caulk, food packaging, and some adhesives. Acrylamide is also found in cigarette smoke…not surprised there.

Acrylamide is formed when certain, particularly **starchy**, foods are cooked at temperatures above about 250° F. 'Starchy' largely means bread and potatoes for most of us to watch out for.

Cooking at these seemingly low temperatures causes a chemical reaction between certain sugars and an amino acid (asparagine) in the food, which creates acrylamide. Cooking these foods at HIGH temperatures often associated with frying in oil causes a much GREATER chemical reaction.

Cooking certain foods using methods such as frying, baking, broiling, or roasting are more likely to create acrylamide because of extremely high temperatures, while boiling, steaming, and microwaving are less likely to do so. It's the darkened, 'burned' bread and potato that's bad to ingest.

In other words, there is a huge difference in how healthy a plate of hash browns is compared to an equal amount of mashed potatoes. Both delicious, but one is loaded with cancer-causing acrylamide.

People who work in certain industries (particularly in the paper and pulp, construction, foundry, oil drilling, textiles, cosmetics, food processing, plastics, mining, and agricultural industries) may be exposed to acrylamide in the workplace, mainly through skin contact or by breathing it in.

I don't know how many MILES of caulk I've applied in my lifetime, but if there was ever a journeyman "Caulker", I'm it lol. And you can't do a professional job at it with protective gloves on! If it's 'finish' caulking then it has to be perfect or I'm not doing it so I've never worn gloves when wiping down thousands of tubes of caulk over my lifetime in construction...geez.

Government regulations are supposed to (!) limit exposure in these settings via the EPA and the Occupational Safety and Health Administration (OSHA). However, there is no warning and no limit to the exposure one can find themselves in when in the public arena, living your life.

You probably didn't know all these acrylamide bullets have been coming at you all your life, I sure didn't. Now I'm dodging them artfully!! ☺

So where have our loving, caring government agencies been at after all this was made public in 2002? It took the citizens of California themselves to rally and warn their fellow residents with Prop 65!

Oh wait, what's this...?

Seems the useless, corrupt alphabet boyz **have** looked into this....and then did nothing.

The National Toxicology Program (NTP) was formed in 1978 from parts of several different US government agencies, including the National Institutes of Health (NIH), the Centers for Disease Control and Prevention (CDC), and the Food and Drug Administration (FDA).

In 2014, the NTP released its Report on Carcinogens for that year. That was the year the NTP classified acrylamide as **"reasonably anticipated to be a human carcinogen"** based on the studies in lab animals.

No warning was issued to the public unless you were a subscriber to NTP Monthly.... (joking). I'm sure they shared the info around their inner circles like they do, and you're left up to some construction worker in his spare time up in Washington state pecking away at a keyboard to sound the alarm....great.

Not sure why the US Environmental Protection Agency (EPA) wasn't involved with the NTP but independently does their own work on toxic substances. The EPA maintains something called the Integrated Risk Information System (IRIS), which is an electronic database that contains information on human health effects from exposure to various substances in the environment.

In 1992, prior to knowing food contained it, the EPA classified acrylamide as **"likely to be carcinogenic to humans"** based on studies in lab animals.

This is unbelievable. In the United States, the FDA regulates the amount of residual acrylamide in a variety of materials that could come in contact with food, **but there are currently no regulations on the presence of acrylamide in food itself whose acrylamide content is off the chart compared to the maximum FDA threshold of a Tupperware container!**

What does the 'F' in FDA stand for again??? I can think of plenty of words that start with F that would fit just fine!! Way better than 'Food' that's for damn sure.

In 2016, the FDA finally issued guidelines to help the food industry reduce the amount of acrylamide in certain foods, **but these are recommendations, not regulations. The fast-food companies, potato chip companies, cereal companies etc. are left to figure it out on their own! These are multi-billion-dollar international corporations who have no intention of doing ANYTHING that would hurt their bottom line.**

If the FDA won't or can't regulate the amount of acrylamide in pre-prepared foods at least warn the damn people!! You know me, I'm not for more government intrusion at all, but I would surely like to see warnings like Prop 65 on every container of McDonalds French fries!! On everything actually, because the burger bun is completely brown top and bottom. The chicken nuggets are completely encased in acrylamide. At least give the people the information for god sakes. And that's across the board, including frozen fries you'd buy at the supermarket, bread like I found that one time...ONE time.

So, what are we looking at in terms of what products to beware of? If you're a junk-food-junkie you better pay attention...

These particular highly-popular foods are more likely to contain acrylamide than others: breads, potato products, especially French fries and potato chips, coffee (!), and foods made from grains like breakfast cereals and cookies.

I have also seen studies suggesting that dietary acrylamide may play a role in Alzheimer's, contributing just one of many hazardous substances thought to bring about the disease. Aluminum from vaccines, deodorants, etc. is also a suspected contributor to the rapidly rising plague of Alzheimer's in our country so again it's a cocktail of toxicity in your body from the globalist multinational corporations that are doing us all in.

Do you think Wonder Bread or Lay's will be beating down our doors to warn us about their products? Hell no! Guard up people.

Let's briefly take a look at one of the most beloved foods in the world: French Fries.

Yeah, I still eat fries, just not nearly as much as before finding all this out!

I guess the old saying is true: Everything will give you cancer!!!

Acrylamide notwithstanding, fast food French fries are typically saturated with trans fats, loaded with sodium and full of simple carbs, which are the bad kind. They are also full of acrylamide. That nice golden coating around the white innards of a French fry...mmmmm.... yummy plastic.... it sure makes it taste good...ugh.

Under something called the Delaney Clause, which amended the federal Food, Drug and Cosmetic Act in 1958, no substance that causes cancer in either humans or animals can be added to food. It sure doesn't seem they enforce the law very well thanks to lobbyists, but that particular law only applies to substances introduced to food as an ingredient, like dyes and preservatives, not those, like acrylamide, created by cooking in a deep fryer.

Since you can't prevent its formation during the deep-frying process, the food industry wants acrylamide treated differently from added food chemicals...even though the acrylamide is technically 'added' to the food before it gets to you. Before potatoes are fried, they have a set amount of ingredients: potato and oil. After frying they have an added ingredient, which is acrylamide.

Again, this certainly isn't meant to be a full report on the dangers associated with acrylamide, but a warning to my readers to research this further. I'll leave you with this news article I came across from Great Britain in the UK's Daily Mail Online, January 24, 2017:

McDonald's reduces cancer risk chemical in their fries: Fast food chain has controls on storage and cooking of potatoes

Fast food companies including McDonald's are taking steps to reduce levels of a cancer-risk chemical in their fries.

All the major chains, including KFC and Burger King, have been told by the Food Standards Agency of the dangers of acrylamide. (FSA is the European equivalent of the United States' FDA)

The agency has this week issued warnings about levels of the chemical in fried and toasted food, as well as crisps, biscuits and baby food.

Acrylamide forms on starchy food such as potatoes and bread when they are roasted, fried, baked or toasted at high temperatures.

Skinny fries are likely to have more acrylamide than chunky chips because they have a greater surface area. McDonald's has responded by introducing controls on the storage and cooking of the potatoes and fries it sells.

At the same time, the British Hospitality Association has issued guidelines to restaurants, pubs and hotels on how to curtail levels of acrylamide.

Importantly, storing potatoes in the fridge leads to a process known as cold sweetening, which increases the levels of acrylamide caused during cooking.

Bosses at McDonald's in the UK have reduced acrylamide to low levels by using varieties of potato that have less starch and so are less likely to generate the chemical.

They are making sure they are not stored in cold conditions and they are capping the temperature used to cook fries. McDonald's said: 'Food safety is a top priority of ours and we have worked with national and European authorities and extensively with our suppliers, taking into consideration a number of factors to mitigate its formation, including the careful selection of potato varieties, storage and processing conditions.

'This extends to preparation in our restaurants where cooking is below a specific temperature – seen as the most important measure in controlling this natural reaction.'

The BHA is working with the FSA to develop a best practice guide that will be published in the summer. It will be used by restaurants, cafes and caterers to minimize acrylamide in fried and roasted foods.

In the meantime, it has issued advice to members that includes cooking foods to light rather than dark colors, frying at lower temperatures for shorter times, and blanching potatoes before frying them to remove some of the starch.

The Mail reported yesterday on the link between baby food and cancer

It says they should avoid storing potatoes in the fridge or using ones which are bruised.

The decision by the FSA to issue warnings to consumers, manufacturers and food chains about the dangers of acrylamide has triggered controversy.

Some academics argue the evidence of harm to human health from acrylamide is 'extremely weak' and does not justify such a public health campaign.

The FSA says it is responding to the findings of the International Agency for Research on Cancer, which has defined the chemical as "probably carcinogenic in humans". The World Health Organization says exposure to the chemical in food 'indicates a human health concern'.

Steve Wearne, director of policy at the FSA, said: 'All age groups have more acrylamide in their diet than we would ideally want.

'As a general rule of thumb when roasting or toasting, people should aim for a golden yellow color, possibly a bit lighter, when cooking starchy foods like potatoes and bread.

'We are not saying avoid any one particular food, or group of foods, but rather people should eat a varied diet. This is about managing risk across a whole lifetime.'

Sucralose

We talked about the dangers of aspartame in my first book, and hopefully you looked into not only that but other artificial sweeteners as they are all poisonous. The best thing for your body if you are looking for something sweet are Yah's natural sweeteners such as non-processed cane sugar, honey, maple syrup and others....Hallelu**YAH**!

Sucralose popped front and center onto my radar thanks to a meme not long after releasing my first book. The information listed on the meme about the dangers of sucralose was shocking. I immediately looked into it and sure enough it's basically a hazmat in your chewing gum, in your diet soda or in a nice little packet on the restaurant table for your coffee.

It's in those little yellow packets on the table in your local restaurant with the packets of processed sugar (white packet), aspartame/Nutrasweet/ Equal (blue packet), and saccharin/Sweet N' Low (pink packet).

Since saccharin had a bad reputation coming out of the 1970s as a probable carcinogen, and people were starting to gain weight due to the rapid rise in processed foods, artificial sweeteners were suddenly in high demand for the battle against the bulge going into the 80s when everyone was moving fast and trying to look their best.

Enter our old nemesis aspartame in 1983 to fill the new demand...

Since the introduction of artificial sweeteners, it seems that peoples' health in general and particularly their weight have gotten progressively worse instead of better for having ingested all that poison.

It seems a lot more people today as opposed to the 1980s and prior look unhealthy....out of shape....overweight....slouching...looking and dressed like something out of a cartoon-with-a-hockey-puck-in-your-stretched-out-ear-gauge-and-a-fish-hook-in-your-lip-and-nose-tacklebox-looking... AAAAHHH...don't get me started!!

People looking to live healthier in the 80s started flocking to artificial sweeteners in droves...all the way to today.

Now you can find **_both_** toxic aspartame and sucralose often TOGETHER in diet sodas, chewing gum, candy, 'healthy and low-fat' processed foods and a host of other products billed as healthy or low-carb or even carb-free.... what a world!

Sure, they have a sweet taste moderately similar to cane sugar but at what cost? It seems sucralose would be better off avoided altogether instead of indulging in a hazmat sweet treat. I'll drink a soda now and then, but I'm looking for a cane sugar soda, otherwise it's not sugar-sweetened but high-fructose corn syrup---which should be included here in Methods of Madness II but there you go, something for you on your own. That crap is AWFUL also.

Within some health circles the dangers of aspartame are now widely known, but still largely unknown by the public judging by the sales of products such as Diet Coke. The risks of using sucralose are not nearly as well known, as it is a newer product and therefore not been around long enough for people like me to pick it apart and warn people about it.

Here's something for you to ponder: **Since sucralose was originally created _with the intent of using it as a pesticide_, our guard instantly goes up!!**

"Splenda" is the brand name for sucralose, and Splenda's marketing slogan is '*Made from sugar so it tastes like sugar*'.

That's funny that they can get away with saying that, because sucralose is nothing like real sugar.

After the sugar is chemically transformed to sucralose it is then factually and scientifically classified as an "organochloride", and organochlorides are notoriously poisonous.

The process by which sugar/sucrose is transformed into Splenda/sucralose involves changing sugar at the molecular level, swapping out natural atoms with chlorine atoms. Chlorine is a known carcinogen so you know this isn't going to end well!!

Why does the FDA allow toxic materials to be used in our food and beverages? You already know the answer to that question: Lobbyists bought and paid for the FDA approval and keep it approved through said ~~bribes~~ lobbying.

The United States Food and Drug Administration approved the use of sucralose in specific food categories in 1998, then expanded the approval to all food and beverage categories in 1999. This product was approved for human consumption despite pre-approval studies showing it was probably toxic!!

Sucralose was originally thought to be biologically inert, at least that's what the corrupted sucralose studies showed. That means it's supposed to pass through the human body unprocessed and THAT'S how it gets its 'zero calorie' claim. Your body doesn't know what to do with it so it doesn't break it down/digest it and just expels it…or so they said.

There have since been recent studies on sucralose, including one in the Journal of Toxicology and Environmental Health from 11/12/13, that are showing that some of the ingested sweetener **IS** in fact metabolized, meaning that it is **NOT** inert. Earlier studies, the ones the FDA used for approval, claimed that sucralose WAS inert and would pass right through the human body unchanged.

It's this kind of treachery why the USA has top-tier doctors and hospitals/healthcare and at the same time the unhealthiest population on the planet… it's caused by the NWO vultures to be that way.

It actually appears that approximately 15% of sucralose on average is processed by the human body…on AVERAGE. This means some people are absorbing it more than 15%, and it seems the healthier a person is the more they uptake it…perfect. That is, it appears that the healthier your gastrointestinal system is, the more sucralose you will absorb into your body.

There have been no long-term studies of sucralose required or even advised by the FDA...as usual it's left up to the multinational corporations to regulate themselves.

So now we've got aspartame's little brother sucralose being used in more than 4,500 products. Oops, did I say little brother? Sucralose is now the #1 selling artificial sweetener in the United States.

So this "Splenda" doesn't do anything to curb your craving for sweets. If anything, it emboldens it and CAUSES weight gain...which artificial sweeteners are supposed to prevent to start with! You can power down tons of food with Splenda, sure there are no sugar calories but what about the carbs!!!

In 2016, The Center for Science in the Public Interest, which is NOT under the thumb of the globalist cabal, recently downgraded their safety rating of sucralose from 'caution' to 'avoid'...not a bad idea and thanks for that!

And here we go again with the fact that these artificial sweeteners cannot be used for cooking because high temperatures cause unwanted chemical reactions just like aspartame!

You know what happens to aspartame when it's heated from my first book, it turns into ethanol and then is broken down into formaldehyde as your body processes it. You're literally embalming yourself from the inside out when you eat aspartame. You know aspartame, right? Ever heard of NutraSweet? Of course, it used to be in everything. Now they switched a ton of consumer products over to Splenda/sucralose.

OK, so what happens to Splenda when it is heated during cooking? It just flat out disintegrates, leaving behind chloropropanes as waste. And what are chloropropanes you might be wondering? Nothing to worry about, they're just DIOXINS...unreal!

This was published in the Journal of Toxicology and Environmental Health in 2013 for your reference.

"Dioxin" is what made Agent Orange so effective at killing plant life, and anything else it touched. The pictures I've seen of the deformed children left in the aftermath of the Vietnam War's use of Agent Orange have been burned into my brain forever as I've researched good ol' Monsanto, the maker of Agent Orange.

Sucralose sounds like a perfect natural sugar substitute to me, something you'd want your kids to eat...no? How about HELL NO.

Sucralose has also been found to kill off the good bacteria in your stomach you need in order to survive! It throws your body's natural balance out of whack stressing your system, which further contributes to cancer among other major health issues.

There are other side effects also, including triggering glucose intolerance, which paves the way for diabetes.

And it's in thousands of our food and drink products, not to mention you can buy a canister of this stuff and just dump it all over your food, put it in drinks or better yet bake a cake with it and create some tasty dioxins.

"But it's FDA approved", you might be saying to yourself if you're not awake to the Great Plan. I know you wouldn't say that, friend, but people you know sure will.

You can immediately tell them that this is the same FDA that miraculously didn't see how globalist-stalwart Merck's 'Vioxx' would go on to kill 55,000 people either! We already went over that in a previous report, but come on, man. (!)

This is the exact same corrupt FDA who is going to rubber stamp the upcoming Covid-19 vaccine...with no financial fault liability to the vaccine maker thanks to the Vaccine Injury Act of 1986! This is MADNESS.

The FDA are as bought-and-paid-for as all our politicians and the rest of the upper echelons of government.

CANE SUGAR. HONEY. MAPLE SYRUP. MOLASSES. Look for it. Learn to use it. Love it in moderation like you should. Just like Yah intended. Not this *manmade* **CRAP**, it's just poison mate!

Brominated Vegetable Oil

There are so many toxic substances lying in wait for you when you enter a convenience store it's unnerving to someone who is awake. There is arguably not a single thing in that convenience store that is good for you if you look into it. Even most of the bottled waters are contaminated with fluoride among other things. I guess that's what happens when most of them are bottled right out of city municipal water supplies....just look on the label!

My favorite convenience store item for many years in my 20s and 30s was a giant fountain Mountain Dew. Used to be nothing like it on a hot day. Taking a lunch break from the 90+ degree dusty jobsite and heading for AM/PM at light speed. A 48 oz. Mountain Dew and a couple of rubber-chicken sandwiches to go!

I used to drink a lot of Mountain Dew...the combo of sugar and caffeine was ideal before all these energy drinks started coming out....it was the original energy drink!

I bought thousands of cups of fountain Mountain Dew right up to 2013. I had just ventured onto Facebook after releasing my first book and was in meme heaven! That's right, another meme to tip me off, which I why I spread memes about the NWO like a madman on social media. Memes really are great for spreading facts and waking people up.

One of the memes took me out at the knees though...it told the truth about my beloved Mountain Dew...

It turns out that Mountain Dew contains Brominated Vegetable Oil (BVO) and it's a **HIGHLY TOXIC** substance to ingest. If you want to suppress a fire though, you sure can't beat it! If you want a fireproof mattress, BVO is the ticket too. Commercially, BVO is a top-notch fire suppressant.

Apparently with a citrus-flavored soda, a means to keep the citrus oil flavoring suspended in the soda was needed or it would separate out. You know what happens when you shake a carbonated beverage so that option was out from the get-go, but BVO solved the problem...albeit it is toxic to consume. The soda 'Squirt' also contains BVO, as well as most if not all generic citrus sodas...and also Gatorade, Powerade, etc. in their citrus flavors.

Now, with all the chemicals I've inhaled or gotten on my skin...in all my decades of construction, that's the last thing I needed to find out in 2013 after waking up to the New World Order: That I've been drinking tons of poisonous fire retardant for the last 30 years.

~~They don't put BMO in Mountain Dew in other countries. Only here in the United States. Why? Right back to the Great Plan to destroy the United States in particular from within.~~

Sorry, that last statement was from my first book in 2013. In 2020 Mountain Dew went BVO-free. Great. Fine. Thanks for that. So what about the 30+ years I drank it when it had it? Haven't drank it since 2013 and especially now never will again, I'm so done.

Fool me once...

Aluminum

Aluminum, like so many other things, can be both good and bad, it just depends on how it is used.

Aluminum is good for things like airplanes, recyclable cans, building materials, etc. It's lightweight and very strong, and very abundant.

Aluminum is bad for things like vaccine ingredients, cookware... and deodorant.

We're not talking about eating, drinking, breathing or even willfully injecting aluminum here though.

We're talking about direct absorption through the skin and into the body in the name of "personal hygiene" by applying aluminum daily to the underarm area, effectively coating your armpits with aluminum grease.

These 'deodorants' and 'anti-perspirants' as a concept were sold to the world in the early 20th century and now close to $5 billion a year is spent in the United States annually on these toxic products.

The first consumer deodorant was introduced in 1888. Deodorants mask/kill the odor-causing bacteria but do not stop perspiration, which is where antiperspirants come in, using aluminum as their active ingredient.

The first consumer antiperspirants were introduced in the early 1900s.

Antiperspirants inhibit sweat-production, which cuts off the food supply for the smelly bacteria that necessitate a deodorant.

Before 1888 you and your B.O. were basically on your own to do something about it.

Most did nothing and it was accepted by society that people are animals by nature and through certain natural body processes you would often have an odor about you.

Society was wary about applying these new and unknown chemicals to their underarms...and rightfully so... that is until the Roaring 1920s rolled around.

So, what happened in the 20s to cause people to buy into using these new, toxic products? Corporate America began advertising to push their 'new' products and the mind programming began.

Advertisements warned women in particular that their armpits might stink like body odor and they might not even know it. Surely the fashionable lady of the Roaring Twenties wouldn't want to be caught smelling foul...at least that's how they sold it...and they bought into it hook, line and sinker.

With advertising in place and growing yearly, so did the norm of using deodorant daily for both sexes. It immediately took off and now nearly everyone has been conditioned to use this product.

Now being a man and a construction worker, I can tell you for a fact that if I don't use deodorant, I have some pretty wicked underarm BO, a sour and surely 'offensive' odor even to me!

I used aluminum-based antiperspirant/deodorant for most of my life.... that is until I woke up to the Great Plan's agenda to make everyone sick to keep us down.

Now I use aluminum, paraben, phthalate, and fragrance-free deodorant by Arm & Hammer. It's not perfect but it works and I cut a bunch of the toxicity out of the equation. My deodorant still has propylene glycol in it so it's not as healthy as using nothing at all.

So here we are in 2020 and we've come full circle. People are starting to question the multitude of toxic ingredients in not only deodorants, but hair sprays, skin creams, etc. and figuring out that we might not have to apply these chemicals to ourselves daily in order to not stink, look good, smell good, etc.

If I'm sitting at a desk plinking away at a book all day I don't sweat and don't need pit stick so I won't put it on that day to cut back as many chemicals as I can I'm coming into contact with. If I'm working hard and sweating on a remodel job, I definitely need something to at least mask my funk for my customer's sake!

At this point I'm sure you know that every day as a targeted citizen of the United States you're exposed to thousands of toxins and chemicals in what we use, wear, eat, drink, breathe, etc.

There are over 10,000 chemical ingredients, some of them known or suspected to cause cancer, in soaps, shampoos, lotions, make-up and beauty products, and other assorted personal care products.

One of the most harmful consumer products out there that both men and women use by putting on their skin to be directly absorbed into the bloodstream is standard-issue deodorant.

If you know about the Great Plan, this is a dream-product for us to use to make us sick and possibly kill us off.

Our bodies sweat to cool us off, yes, but we also sweat to discharge toxins out of our bodies. Antiperspirant **is a product that inhibits your body's natural secretion of toxins** by literally **CLOGGING** your underarm **skin follicles** so that you're not able to sweat as much.

On top of inhibiting your body's natural cleansing and detoxifying process, deodorants and antiperspirants also release a myriad of harmful chemicals into our bodies through simple skin-absorption.

Aluminum being sprayed in the air against our will via chemtrails and getting into everything we eat, drink and breathe is one thing, but people are willingly applying aluminum paste and a host of other noxious chemicals to their skin, absorbing it into their bodies, and developing breast cancer, Alzheimer's Disease and other ailments ever more frequently as a result.

When you eat something, it has to get by the body's main poison-filtering system, the liver. When something is smeared on your skin it absorbs directly into the bloodstream, bypassing the liver, and heads straight for your brain, heart and breasts among other major organs.

Aluminum-based compounds are the principal active ingredient in antiperspirants. These aluminum-based compounds form a temporary "plug" within the sweat duct to stop-up flow of sweat to the skin's surface, literally blocking the sweat duct. Knowing what I know that doesn't sound like a healthy thing to do!

Aluminum exposure has been linked with the development of Alzheimer's disease. Not only this, but the fluoride in the water that most people drink in the U.S. reacts with aluminum in the body causing it to be even more destructive to one's health!

Aluminum in antiperspirants is also known to accumulate in breast tissue and may be linked to an increased cancer risk, particularly to women.

Aluminum is known to interfere with estrogen receptors and levels in breast cancer cells in particular, and when your body can't process estrogen properly there's a higher risk for breast cancer in women and prostate cancer in men.

Since aluminum's main function is to "block" your sweat glands, what happens to all of that sweat? With your underarms being in close proximity with your lymph nodes, this accumulation of toxic load from the sweat that isn't being perspired is causing biologic mayhem underneath that pit of yours.

No build-up of toxin is ever good for the body and long-term buildup can easily contribute to onset of cancer.

Moving on down the line of ingredients that the deodorant I currently use **DOESN'T** have, but most others do, are something called parabens.

Parabens are preservatives used in deodorants and antiperspirants that also mimic the activity of estrogen in the body's cells.

By acting as an added, synthetic estrogen, parabens are particular contributors to the onset of both breast and prostate cancer.

In both women AND men, there is estrogen-sensitive tissue in the breast area. By applying paraben-laced deodorant DAILY to your underarm you are putting this breast tissue in direct contact with parabens.

I came across one study from 2012 that showed out of 160 tissue samples from 40 mastectomies, 99% of the samples contained parabens!

The third ingredient that my personal deodorant is missing are "phthalates".

Phthalates are listed under the ingredients as "fragrance", but are really there for their ability to help dissolve the other ingredients, keeping them semi-fluid and helping to dispense the spray/roll-on deodorant.

When you put phthalates on your skin they are immediately absorbed into your system and, yet again, these substances act as _estrogens_.

Phthalates are associated with the following health conditions: Infertility, decreased sperm count, cancers of all sorts, liver/kidney/lung damage, endometriosis, asthma, and allergies.

Phthalates are not only in deodorants but a host of other skin-care products so if you're a woman reading this BEWARE!

The one ingredient that I know is in my Arm & Hammer Essentials Unscented that isn't good is propylene glycol.

When used daily, propylene glycol can cause damage to your nervous system, liver and heart. About 50% of that stick of deodorant is pure propylene glycol. It is the #1 ingredient, including my 'natural' deodorant.

Propylene glycol acts as a skin penetration-enhancer and when paired with toxic chemicals like aluminum and phthalates it greatly increases their absorption into your bloodstream.

Propylene glycol all by itself has been linked to cancer, reproductive complications, developmental issues and neurotoxicity. Pair that with a half-dozen other toxic chemicals and no wonder the cancer rates have exploded in the United States in the 20th century and beyond to today.

There are a host of other toxic ingredients in deodorants, including stearates, triclosan, triethanolamine (TEA) and diethanolamine (DEA), and "artificial colors". "Artificial colors" is a catch-all for anything else they want to throw in there and not list the actual ingredient!

Again, if I'm not leaving the house on any particular day I don't put on deodorant.

Remember, this is just ONE consumer product that is used daily and contains all these poisons. Add in some fluoridated water, GMO food, artificial sweeteners, etc. and we are navigating a minefield of toxicity on a daily basis.

Glyphosate

When it comes to the popular consumer and agricultural product glyphosate, going by the brand name 'Roundup', by the time the aftermath of side effects of its use started showing up it seems the damage had already been done to mankind by Monsanto...as usual.

This has happened time and time again, and since Monsanto was swallowed up by Bayer AG a couple years ago, their financial prowess is off the chart, making them virtually untouchable...and unstoppable.

Remember, Monsanto is the globalist company that invented saccharin, PCBs, Agent Orange, aspartame, synthetic Bovine Growth Hormone (rBGH), GMO foods and of course, Roundup.

Monsanto was in the news quite a bit there a couple years ago when they lost that huge settlement to the groundskeeper in California who came down with non-Hodgkin lymphoma from using and coming into contact with Roundup.

In August 2018 Monsanto lost in court after it was factually proven that using Roundup can and does cause cancer, something Monsanto denied for *decades.*

The groundskeeper, Dewayne Johnson, was awarded $292 million initially, but came down on appeals to $78.5 million, and then down more thanks to Monsanto attorneys to $20 million.

The attorneys claimed that he didn't need all that money because he didn't have much longer to live!! Unreal.

They have literally been getting away with murder for DECADES at this point.

Right before the jury's verdict, in June 2018, Bayer bought Monsanto.

Yeah, THAT Bayer from an earlier update! Demons of a feather flock together right? Right.

That's why Bill Gates divested his holdings in Microsoft and bought millions of dollars' worth of Monsanto years ago!

By purchasing Monsanto, Bayer was able to keep Monsanto's products and ditch the notorious name.

Most people have a naively favorable opinion of Bayer because everyone has heard of and used Bayer aspirin for generations.

The amount of money they make on Roundup alone makes the $20 million dollar judgement a farce, barely a slap on the wrist.

Before they 'vanished', Monsanto was widely considered to be the most evil and diabolical corporation on the planet...second only to Bill Gates' Microsoft...natch.

Monsanto has been sued 6 ways from Sunday on all of its past and current products and the litigation continues today. In particular, if you look up the litigation regarding Agent Orange and the toxic dioxins it contained you will find they killed hundreds of thousands and maimed millions with this abominable substance during the Vietnam War.

They knew this stuff was toxic, lied to the government at the time, and lied about their internal findings in lawsuits through the 70s and 80s.

This all came to light in a trial in 2002, an internal memo was made public about what Monsanto knew about Agent Orange but denied in court up to this point when they were caught red-handed:

"that the evidence proving the persistence of these compounds and their universal presence as residues in the environment is beyond question ... the public and legal pressures to eliminate them to prevent global contamination are inevitable. The subject is snowballing. Where do we go from here? The alternatives: go out of business; sell the hell out of them as long as we can and do nothing else; try to stay in business; have alternative products."

Does the term 'global contamination' sound concerning? They are talking about Agent Orange here in this instance.

How about 'alternative products'???

Now many years later, humanity is in this exact problem with a completely different product from ~~Monsatan~~ Monsanto called Roundup, and we are exactly at the global contamination phase now!!

Glyphosate, the 'active' ingredient in Roundup, is now factually proven to be found in almost all foods, beverages, the air, water, land and everything!!

It has contaminated the entire planet, literally and factually, and it's use increases like clockwork every year despite all the red flags going up everywhere that we've got to stop this madness.

Those useless eaters over at the UN banging the drum over non-existent, man-made climate change won't even bat an eye at Roundup because this is part of the Great Plan to destroy us by making us too sick to fight back.

In the ten-year span of 2008 to 2018, an estimated 6.1 billion kilograms of Monsanto's proven carcinogen 'Roundup' were applied to the surface of the Earth.

Quick math says that for every single person on the planet, just under one kilogram of cancer-causing Roundup went into our environment, into the air, soil and groundwater supplies.

Let's quickly get up to speed with regards to Roundup, where it came from, and where we're going with this nightmare, because our federal, state and local government have failed us MISERABLY on this.

Where in the hell is the Department of Ecology on this…keep reading!!

Roundup is the most widely used agricultural chemical in **history**, but it didn't get its start in agriculture.

It was originally patented in 1961 as a de-scaling agent for cleaning up calcium and other mineral deposits in pipes and boilers!! Try spraying it on the hard-water spots on your shower tile or glass, it will probably clean them like new!! Make sure to wear a hazmat suit though because this stuff is really that toxic.

Nine years later in 1970, Monsanto discovered glyphosate was an effective weed killer and was immediately patented as such and brought to market in 1974 under the trade name 'Roundup'.

It was a modest success but Monsanto had big plans for the future of glyphosate as a corporate cash-cow. Their sinister plan was to create genetically-modified crops they would call 'Roundup Ready' that would withstand the effects of Roundup while allowing everything else it touched to wither and die.

Monsanto's first success at genetic modification for plants to resist Roundup came in 1985 when they created petunia plants that could withstand small amounts of Roundup, but not the kind of quantities needed to effectively farm with a financial dependence on Roundup.

Since Roundup/Glyphosate is such a toxic chemical, Monsanto themselves had a bit of trouble getting the genetic modifications right in order to bring the new strains of plants they were seeking to market so they brought on outside help to get their GMO corn and soybean strains to market.

In 1996 we had the introduction to the food chain of "Roundup Ready Soybeans". That first year of planting, Roundup accounted for approximately 3.8% of the total amount of herbicide used in United States agriculture. Approximately 28 million pounds went into the environment that year.

Monsanto, always looking to drive up profits no matter the danger to humanity, also encouraged farmers of non-GMO crops to use Roundup as a 'desiccant', meaning **the naïve farmers were encouraged to spray Roundup on their crops as they came mature to kill them and dry them out in place, THEN harvest these Roundup-laden, non-GMO crops for market!**

This practice happens even today to crops such as non-GMO wheat, barley, oats, canola, flax, peas, lentils, soybeans, dry beans and sugar cane.

Doesn't do much good to buy non-GMO if it's been soaked in cancer-causing Roundup…ugh. We are getting attacked at every turn today.

I am so pissed right now writing all this down and reading it over and over as I'm editing!!! My blood is literally boiling right now at 12:45 PM PST 11/15/2020 as I'm doing the final edit. This truly is Satan's world.

Ok. So ten years after introducing GMO soybeans in 2007, Monsanto had added more GMO vegetables to their merchandising arsenal and Roundup was now being applied nationwide at the rate of 185 million pounds per year.

By 2014 annual Roundup application in the USA alone had increased to approximately 240 million pounds, that's closing in on one pound per person in the USA…annually! Every damn year! A pound per person being dumped into our environment. No wonder it's in everything up and down the food chain.

Finally, in 2015, the World Health Organization's cancer agency IARC sounded the alarm as it couldn't be ignored anymore, and classified glyphosate as "probably carcinogenic to humans". This was the tipping point of humanity finally starting to wake up to this insanity.

Now the independent researchers could smell smoke, and where there's smoke, there's fire.

In 2016, University of California San Francisco (UCSF) researchers discovered that glyphosate was in **93% of urine samples collected across USA**. 93% of people tested positive for Roundup in their system!!

It suddenly started becoming apparent that glyphosate was seeping and creeping into all avenues of mankind's existence, including mankind himself!

In November of 2016, "The Detox Project" and "Food Democracy Now!" jointly announced that alarming levels of glyphosate were being found in many popular foods including Kellogg's cereals, Doritos, Ritz crackers and a number of other popular foods.

In 2017 researchers announced that **low** doses of Roundup caused liver disease at thousands of times below what is permitted by the United States EPA.

Also, in 2017, came the litigation...finally. Internal Monsanto and EPA communications that were released during Roundup-related cancer court cases revealed the facts of the 30+ year glyphosate cover-up.

The internal company e-mails showed how Monsanto **had colluded with the EPA behind the scenes to diminish glyphosate safety concerns**, and admitted that Roundup could possibly cause cancer and a host of other diseases.

In July 2019, Austria became the first country to ban Roundup. Finally, some sanity!

Monsanto originally claimed their GMO crops would reduce pesticide and herbicide use but the amount of Roundup used only goes up every year!

They have falsified data on Roundup's safety, claimed it is safe and 'environmentally friendly', and encouraged its use on playgrounds, golf courses, schoolyards and of course around our own homes' lawns and gardens where our children and pets hang out and play...and live.

Even though in recent years it has been found that Roundup is vastly more toxic than what was presented to the feds back in the 70s, this has not led to any regulatory changes by the EPA or FDA in regards to Roundup... NOTHING. Again, we've been failed, victims of the Great Plan.

Overuse of Roundup has now contributed to weeds building up immunity and having to apply even more and concentrated Roundup, dumping even more toxicity into the food chain. I think there are 2 or 3 different levels of concentration of Roundup these days. This has to stop, this is flippin' insane.

To sum up, it has been found that the following health problems can be partially if not completely attributed to glyphosate exposure, and we are virtually ALL contaminated with it, in our bodies, right this second: ADHD, Alzheimer's, Anencephaly, Autism, birth defects, cancer of all sorts, Celiac disease, chronic kidney disease, Colitis, depression, diabetes, gluten intolerance, heart disease, hypothyroidism, IBS, liver disease, Lou Gehrig's Disease, Multiple Sclerosis, Non-Hodgkin lymphoma, Parkinson's, pregnancy issues, obesity, reproductive problems and finally respiratory illness.

It probably would have been easier to list the diseases Roundup DOESN'T cause for god sakes!!

The tide is starting to turn. It's up to people like you and me to be waking up others to keep the heat on with regards to Roundup and everything else we're going over in this report, my other reports, and of course my first two books! I would **NEVER** be able to sit on my hands watching my country and my kids' future go up in flames!!

~~Ritalin/Adderall~~ Meth Lite

Everyone has heard of the 'opioid' epidemic and the lawsuits, litigation and multi-billion-dollar settlements over oxycodone/hydrocodone (Vicodin, Percocet, Percodan, and the like), but there is an epidemic that has swept through our country as bad or worse than synthetic opioids, and is a raging inferno today...and virtually nobody is talking about it.

I'm talking about 'meth lite', also known as Ritalin for the kids, and Adderall for the big kids like you and me.

If you want it, there is a doctor who will be happy to prescribe it for a host of "symptoms" and then of course they will get their commission and their bonuses for "selling" it. That's about all doctors are these days, drug salesmen for Big Pharma.

The drug companies made sure to have everyone eligible for prescription meth, kids and adults, which is all these pills are. A lot of doctors are no better than street dealers and arguably worse because the government is on their side protecting this racket!! Collecting tax revenue off of addiction, misery and death! That's the NWO for you....*rolls eyes*.

I was a meth/crank user in my 20s during the 1990s when meth was really catching on, and it came on fast and was everywhere, just like cocaine in the 70s and 80s.

In the 1990s, as crystal meth use exploded nationwide, the drug companies saw this burgeoning, lucrative, and illegal market and figured out a way to sell illegal speed legally, so they started pushing illegal drug substitutes they already had in their arsenal, synthetic heroin and meth. You know these drugs today as Vicodin/Percocet/Percodan and Ritalin/Adderall.

It seems that **illegal** crystal meth wasn't the only thing taking off in the 1990s, that's exactly when **legal** meth (Ritalin) began to be prescribed exponentially to America's youth.

Ritalin was actually approved by the FDA in 1955, and first prescribed to treat ADHD in the early 60s. It seems we didn't have a Ritalin epidemic until crystal meth rose up to popularity in the 1990s and Big Pharma saw dollar signs selling synthetic meth to an easily brainwashable population.

And what better way to sell meth that to convince teachers and parents that ADHD was suddenly an "epidemic".

When I was a kid going to grade school in the 1970s, maybe it's where I went to school, but if you screwed around in class you were liable to get your ass kicked by the teacher or the principal, literally. I saw more than one kid spanked by a teacher in my day!

By the time of the 1990s, physical punishment was no longer PC but prescribing toxic drugs to kids was. No wonder the country is so screwed up! You don't get addicted to a spanking...quite the opposite!!

Getting the kids hooked on Ritalin set the stage for them to continue the drug abuse into their adult years with Adderall, introduced to America after FDA approval in dat-da-da-daaaaa....1996.

If getting Adderall for an adult who was addicted to it was ever an issue in terms of price or availability of funds, there was always crystal meth, which is cheaper and more powerful...and easy to get.

Getting a cheaper and more powerful drug that satisfies your addiction and then some sounds like a no-brainer on more than one front because when you're on any of these hyper-stimulants you are literally OUT OF YOUR FRIKKEN MIND!

Doctors are being paid big bonuses by drug companies to push these drugs just like they do vaccines!!!!! It's not about making you well at all, it's about making you a customer of Big Pharma...which is owned and controlled by behind-the-scenes Illuminati stockholders.

There is a relentless marketing campaign by the government against meth, but on the flip side the same government approves literally legalized meth to be prescribed to children and adults. They don't want the competition of the street meth which isn't taxed and that's the bottom line of it!!!!! Look at all the states now legalizing recreational marijuana...they are only seeing tax dollars. That is the ONLY reason pot is becoming legal across the nation...tax money.

Ritalin, Adderall, etc. and also the synthetic opioids are government-approved, mind-altering drugs that were lobbied through and now the government is making money off of drug dependency via sales tax!!

Adderall and crystal meth are virtually the same in their chemical structure if you look into it, and I encourage you to. One is legal, government-approved and taxed, and one is illegal with possession a felony. Yet they are both virtually the same substance.

Adderall is dextroamphetamine, and crystal meth is methamphetamine.... both amphetamines.

As I was conducting the research for this chapter, I had a random incident occur about legal 'meth'. I was listening to the afternoon drive-time radio show on the local rock music station in Seattle, KISW 99.9, and they were taking calls from people who had various experiences on drugs...any drugs.

A guy called and started talking about his experience being on ADHD drugs, and in particular Adderall. He said that when he's on Adderall, he's fine: tons of energy, stays focused, loss of appetite which keeps his weight under control, etc. He said when he's not on it he's dead to the world: no energy, can't stay focused, eats tons of junk food, etc. He was basically testifying that he was addicted to legal speed and when he's not on it he's like a drug addict and can't function without it. Now, imagine getting your kids on this stuff via Ritalin and having them grow up not knowing any other life than to be addicted to speed? That's where we're at today for MILLIONS of kids and adults.

Conclusion

The liberal/NWO mainstream media bias against Trump, the 'right', the United States, and decency in general is off the charts, they really had it on display for this Presidential election.

Even FOX news showed their true NWO colors and went against Trump which isn't a surprise since the guy calling the shots at FOX now, James Murdoch, son of Rupert Murdoch, gave the Biden campaign $1.5 million!!

You can search for the tweets of James' wife crowing about how they helped beat Trump on Twitter! If you're not done with FOX you better be!

So now the bought-and-paid-for media have crowned Biden the President with no authority to do so and unconditionally sold it to the left that Biden won, that there was no voter fraud, and that he will be sworn in next January... and to celebrate and rejoice because finally orange man gone!!

Nothing could be further from the real truth, and this could easily launch the second Civil War I talked about in the last update!

There is TONS of evidence of voter fraud, Biden HASN'T won because he hasn't been confirmed in a single state, and there is a good chance the courts will declare Trump winner. Remember, the courts look at the facts and will have to rule and be accountable for the facts publicly.

You think you've seen bad rioting...you ain't seen nuthin' yet.

If Trump is declared winner by the courts get out of the major cities as fast as you can because there will be historic rioting, looting, destruction and DEATH, especially in democrat-run cities.

Hundreds or thousands will easily die in the cities if Trump comes out on top after the extreme leftists get the rug jerked out from under them.

IMO, Trump won by a landslide and the NWO is trying to steal this election so they can install their puppets Biden and Harris. If Biden does get in, eventually he will probably bow out and it will be Harris and whoever the Speaker of the House is will be Harris' Veep, time will tell.

I'm pulling for Trump to stay in just to see what happens, and of course to try and hold off the inevitable for a few more years. He's surely the lesser of two evils, not that Trump is evil but at the end of the day he's still a billionaire elitist. The Federal Reserve is still in place. There has been no new, independent 9/11 investigation. The United Nations still operates on United States soil. Hillary isn't in jail. Etc. etc. etc.

The following is excerpted from my first book, "Rise of the New World Order: The Culling of Man", chapter 7/A-Voting Machine Fraud, January 2013:

Let's start off with the people who we "elected" to drive our country straight into the ground....

Campaign donations and clandestine actions from pro-New World Order entities aside, we've got a terrible issue we need to address, and that is a legitimate, factual concern about voting machine fraud. The proponents of the Great Plan have pulled out all the stops to advance their agenda, and have left no avenue uncompromised to complete their mission.

Think about this: The 50 states in the USA are divided into over 3,000 counties. Ohio, for instance, is divided into 88 counties, Iowa is divided into 99 counties, and so on. In approximately 1% of these counties, there are paper ballots which are hand counted properly, the way all of our counties should be counting our ballots. This respectable 1% nationally consists of about half of the counties in New Hampshire alone---the *"Live Free or Die"* state---and a very few, very small counties scattered throughout the rest of the United States.

In 99% of the other compromised counties, the Democratic and Republican controlled Boards of Elections make sure that the ballots are commandeered from the neighborhood precincts as the polls close their doors. This is to make sure that the neighborhood citizens and other watchdog-patriots do NOT have a chance to count, or at least spot-check, their own votes. Such counting or spot-checking by the citizens would make centralized computer vote-rigging impossible. This is why the Illuminati, who today control both the national Democratic and Republican parties through the CFR, vehemently oppose any such citizen participation at the neighborhood precinct level. This is because centralized counting is the common feature of **all** governments trying to rig elections.

"Those who cast the votes decide nothing. Those who count the votes decide everything."
-Joseph Stalin

In these 99% of USA counties, citizens are forced to use either computer or machine methods of casting a ballot. Vote counting is wide open for fraud this way. The Democratic and Republican parties at the county level delegate the "counting" to one of a small handful of privately-owned companies which count 99% of the votes in United States national elections in complete secret, with no independent verification or audit.

Currently the four companies which are delegated the power to count the votes in the USA were Election Systems & Software, Diebold, Hart, and Sequoia. The local county election boards use armed guards to make sure the citizens, candidates, and reporters cannot see what these private companies are doing to the ballots in the "counting room" on election night.

Since 1973, the powers behind the RNC and the DNC have arm-twisted, persuaded, and bullied the local governments in most counties in the USA to unconstitutionally delegate the vote counting to these four mysterious companies. By 1988, the counting companies had consolidated their control over 49 states, and half of New Hampshire.

The private companies controlling the ballots are given a direct feed to a team of manipulators which represent a pool of the AP wire service and the major TV Networks, all under Illuminati control.

The vote-fraud cartel was further empowered through the implementation of the criminal "Help Americans Vote Act" of 2002 or HAVA, which should really be called the "Helping the New World Order by Computer Fraud" Act.

HAVA appropriated **$4 billion** of our money to entice the state and county election offices to implement computer "vote-counting" systems from basically three major companies, Diebold, Sequoia, and Election Systems & Software. These systems provide for no paper trail and no citizen checks and balances. Most people have no idea how their vote is counted, and I'm here to tell you as of right now under this system, your vote doesn't count.

The patriotic organization "Citizens for a Fair Vote Count" has estimated that it would take no more than $400 million dollars per election to hand count every vote on every ballot in the United States. Because the New World Order proponents and their Mainstream Media insist on easily rigged elections, all you hear is how we can't possibly afford the expense of a hand count.

We spend hundreds of BILLIONS of dollars supporting our world military empire. Billions of dollars were just spent on just the promotion and advertising for the 2012 Presidential election alone. Why would billions of dollars be spent for a job that only pays $400,000 year unless someone else besides the President is going to benefit? You already know the answer to that. We can easily fund an honest and accountable vote-counting system by the people, for the people; to ensure that who we want running the country is who gets into power. This is the only way we are going to get our foot in the door and get some real "change" in this country.

So, in a nutshell, it's either paper ballots/hand counting for an honest election and real change, or corrupted centralized computer counting by the proponents of the New World Order and the usual suspects stay in office...over and over and over, pushing our country further and further under water.

Which would you prefer?

Now whether or not Stalin's quote above is legit is up in the air. Back when I researched this book there were no 'fact checkers' running around on social media or even Google to cloud the waters. Now the quote is being called false by some and true by some.

Whether or not the quote is from Stalin is a moot point with regards to what it says, the quote tells the truth as we knew it and now the entire country knows it as this Presidential election is headed for the courts over exactly this: fraudulently altering the election by a company called Dominion.

On November 6 it was revealed that the Dominion election software that Michigan uses to count votes 'glitched' and flipped 6,000 Trump votes to Biden!! They say they fixed it, but this is the same software counting votes in 30 STATES INCLUDING EVERY SINGLE SWING STATE!!!!

Now it is looking like this same situation has happened everywhere, always flipping Trump's votes to Biden, but it will be up to Trump's lawyers and the courts to sort out right now.

There are 2 scenarios coming up that I see and either is possible.

One, Biden will stave off Trump's legal challenges and boom we're off to progress straight into the New World Order.

Or, two, Trump is handed the Presidency by the courts, the left will lose their minds and riot like never before, the corruption of the Democratic Party will be on display like never before, with millions defecting to the conservative side. The mainstream media will have lost all clout with most Americans and the independent media will take off like a rocket.

I'm expecting the first option... and praying for the second!!

If Biden gets in you can expect a full return towards heading into the New World Order. He already said he will immediately sign us back up into the Paris Climate Accord. I'm sure our re-entry into the TPP and WHO won't be far behind. Mandatory masks, contact tracing and vaccine will also come under Biden.

If Trump stays in the sheer number of people who would now be behind him will hopefully empower him to arrest and prosecute the Obamas, Bidens, Clintons, etc....that is, if he's truly on our side...I still just don't know.

I'm sorry to say that if Trump is on our side and successful in the courts and serves a second term, the proponents of the New World Order probably won't let him live long as he's already done a ton of damage to their globalist agenda.

In fact, I would bet that he doesn't make it through 2021 without being killed. I'm sorry to say that but I'm a realist and the track record proves that if you cross the Illuminati and upend the Great Plan you won't last long no matter who you are.

Speaking of crossing the Illuminati and their Great Plan for global domination, since the last update report a little incident called the 'Hunter Biden Laptop' happened right before Election Day.

A coincidence? Surely not on the timing aspect. This laptop has been floating around dark circles for months, even the head of the FBI has been factually sitting on it for months...all the way through the Trump impeachment proceedings!

The contents of this laptop should have been made public then to show everyone who was REALLY conspiring with not only the Ukrainians but the Russians and Chinese...the Bidens! Not only are Joe and Hunter Biden implicated by the contents of the laptop but Joe's brother James Biden also.

There is unbelievable government corruption on that laptop and sadly it also appears that there is a lot of pedophilia-related content involving at least Hunter Biden and possibly (probably) other significant personalities.

The contents of the laptop have been all but dumped on the dark web, I've seen more stills of a naked Hunter Biden in compromising positions than I ever would have thought to have had a nightmare about but they are out there if you want to look. I never get on the dark web, but have seen the stills with the faces and private areas blocked out, some were certainly underage girls.

This information has been completely suppressed by the mainstream media as they are not real reporters but actors working for the globalists and reading from a prepared script for the Great Plan agenda, and if they stray from the 'official story' they will be instantly fired and blacklisted...since all the media is on the same, globalist side now.

These 'reporters' wouldn't be able to make the millions of dollars and get the fame they love anywhere else but working for the pedo-Satanists so they do as they're told, when they're told, or all that money and fame will go away forever. They are just as bought-and-paid-for as our politicians.

Any liberal reporters that tried to do the right thing as 'independent' credible journalists and that dared to touch the laptop story were immediately censored by their seniors. Case in point, the resignation of prominent liberal investigative journalist Glenn Greenwald from The Intercept, an organization he co-founded no less!

Greenwald accused his co-senior editors of censoring an article he wrote, "based on recently revealed emails and witness testimony" that "raised critical questions" about Democrat Joe Biden's conduct in overseas dealings.

On the flip side, the CEOs of Twitter and Facebook were recently subpoenaed in regards to their role in restricting the reach of a NY Post story about Hunter Biden's laptop, the story that broke the laptop scandal.

One of Hunter Biden's former business partners, Anthony Bobulinski, confirmed in a statement to several news outlets that the emails on the laptop implicating the Bidens as corrupt are "genuine", even appearing on FOX's Tucker Carlson show to explain what he knew!

Joe Biden has steadfastly denied any wrongdoing and has "never spoken to my son about his overseas business dealings" ...which is a lie according to the emails and Bobulinski's eyewitness testimony. If he wasn't telling the truth he could be sued for millions for slander by the Bidens.

If you get a chance to watch that particular interview, I highly suggest it and everything else you can research on this topic while you can.

If Biden does get installed as President and goes down over the laptop, Kamala will pardon him and Hunter. If Joe stays in and only Hunter goes down, Joe will pardon him. Odds are since everything is so corrupt that NOTHING will happen to either cretin thanks to the media blocking for them.

Keep a special eye on the Georgia Senate runoffs going forward, if the NWO is able to secure both Senate seats they will be in the driver's seat going forward, able to add Supreme Court Justices to swing the court back to the left...just saying!

Ok. Let's talk briefly about the current and coming plannedemic situation...oh boy....here we go.

Joe Biden said during the last Presidential debate and multiple time since that we have a 'dark winter' coming right up.

Could he have been double speaking by saying this? What does teh internetz say about 'dark winter' as it applies to a pandemic....

"Dark Winter" was the code name for a senior-level bio-terrorist attack drill causing a nationwide smallpox pandemic that was conducted on June 22–23, 2001.

The timing of this exercise sets off severe alarm bells to me since this was only 3 months before 9/11. Was it possible that this was the backup plan to 9/11? Instead of planes hitting on 9/11, a bioterrorist attack to cause a pandemic?

I wouldn't be surprised, the public is so dumbed-down that they would believe a fake alien invasion at this point. Time to brush up on Project Blue Beam 😊

I am still feeling that they will announce the sudden discovery of a mutated version of Covid-19...even if there isn't one just as there is no deadly pandemic right now. The current version of Covid-19 is less deadly than the annual flu and the government is putting us through all this hassle? Mandatory masks and social distancing and blah blah blah. And throwing money at us on top of it to keep us appeased??

This was cut and pasted right off the CDC website. This disease is not deadly at all!!!

"If you test positive for COVID-19, know what protective steps to take if you are sick... *MOST* PEOPLE HAVE *MILD* COVID-19 ILLNESS AND CAN RECOVER AT HOME WITHOUT MEDICAL CARE. Contact your healthcare provider if your symptoms are getting worse or if you have questions about your health."

This whole plannedemic stinks to high hell and it's not going away any time soon, so you need to figure out what you're going to do about it. How to deal with it. People are going to start losing it even more than they are now. Start researching what is happening. The more you know what is factually happening the better because the media completely proved they couldn't be trusted to be non-biased... the election was just the capper!

Well, just keep tabs on what I've got going on and I'll tell you what I know...it's just enough to keep me out of trouble (!)

Now all this mask-wearing everyone is doing is going to probably start a new plague called pneumonia, I'm sure you've heard of it or had it! I've had it and it's no fun!

Let's be honest, we've all had it, bacterial pneumonia, **so why did Dr. Anthony Fauci himself author a paper in 2008 that said that most of the victims of the Spanish Flu didn't die of the virus but of the bacterial pneumonia brought on by constant mask wearing...FACT!**

You've read my second update back in May about Fauci, Baal Gates and the rest of the diabolical mad scientists. None of these people are trustworthy by research and fact.

So now they all are saying that numbers of infected people are going through the roof, which scares more people into getting tested, and all those false positives are thrown onto the statistic pile, which scares more people into getting tested, and on and on and on. See how that works?

More and more people who aren't showing symptoms are getting tested for COVID-19, which results in tons of false positives, some probably are truly positive as Covid-19 is for real and an engineered virus if you remember from update #1 back in March.

Then the media blares out alarming new numbers, which panics more people who don't have symptoms into getting tested, which then causes even more false positives, and the media pukes out those numbers all over the public, panicking them more, and on and on and on.

The PCR test is very flawed, the main test they use for COVID-19. From what Fauci said the people conducting the tests are running some part of it wrong, too many or not enough cycles of something, and this and that and the other thing... it's just a cluster-f, you know? And it's meant to be that way to confuse people so they can capitalize on the confusion. Order out of chaos, remember?

It is my understanding that the inventor of the PCR test himself, Kary Mullis, said it shouldn't be used to test for ANY VIRUS because it's unreliable in that capacity... but he died last year coincidentally and wasn't available for comment...unbelievable!!! So they just keep using the test and send us off to pandemic oblivion.

Pfizer's vaccine results were just published, 90% effective allegedly, against a disease with a 99+% recovery rate and arguably way less dangerous than the seasonal flu.

What are the odds that Pfizer would announce this news just days after Biden 'won'...geez.

Well.....let's see....what else did I come across....oh yeah....(!)

Operation Crimson Contagion was a drill conducted from January to August 2019, just months ahead of our plannedemic...what are the odds!

OCC involved national, state and local, private and public organizations in the United States to try and test (allegedly) the capacity of the federal government and twelve states to respond to a severe pandemic of influenza originating in China.

The simulation revolved around incoming tourists returning from China, bringing a deadly strain of flu home with them. In less than two months the virus was to have infected 110 million Americans, killing more than half a million.

The report concluded that the Federal Government currently had limited capacity to respond to a pandemic, with federal agencies lacking the funds, coordination, and resources to facilitate an effective response to the virus...well DUHHHHHHH!!

And then out of the blue a "pandemic" coincidentally hits...whammo! Sound the alarm!!! A virus we engineered and released is on the loose!! Everyone panic and do as we say or else you'll DIE!!!! That's where we're at right now.

Just like in the aftermath of 9/11 with the Patriot Act and the creation of Homeland Security, if Biden gets in there, there will be another 'Patriot Act' against the public virus and another governmental behemoth like Homeland Security in the form of Pandemic Security or some BS like that... mark my words!

I'm talking about the same government that couldn't even handle a single emergency, Hurricane Katrina. Remember that debacle? They wouldn't be able to handle a nationwide emergency...we're too big! We will certainly be on our own if there is a major calamity and I'm telling you to be prepared.

As of right now, if Trump wins the cities will burn, the BIG cities, and there will be no stopping it because the people who will be doing it will be ARMED this time and looking for blood. They will shoot at the cops and kill them off and the cops will then abandon the cities. Ever seen the movie "Escape from New York"??

The leftist media has conditioned the extreme left to get violent when they want something or don't get their way and this would be the granddaddy of them all...another 4 years of Trump!!

We're in a very dangerous time to be alive as the proponents of the New World Order try to jockey us into position to be fully enslaved with global socialism. That is EXACTLY THE PLAN.

What better way to get us under martial law than to burn down the big cities? Unreal.

So how much more dangerous the disease COVID-19 than the cure?

A largely untested mRNA vaccine from Pfizer? Absolutely NO long-term studies performed yet with regards to this brand-new technology?? Absolutely no liability to Pfizer thanks to the 1986 Vaccine Act? What could possibly go wrong?

This is serious technology, mRNA, that messes with your DNA and they are shoving it down our throat? From a globalist Big Pharma company who can't be trusted worth a damn? Who had the single largest criminal fine ever imposed in the United States, for any matter EVER, handed down against them in 2009 for fraudulent and illegal marketing? Pfizer? And Moderna's vaccine that is coming right up uses the same type of technology. Pfizer and Moderna have the lead on getting a vaccine to market and are the only two out of a dozen or so potential front-running vaccines to use mRNA technology.

These are the two companies' vaccines that will be mandated by LAW that we are all supposed to get so you better research and pipe up right now, sentinels!!

Research mRNA technology NOW because it's coming, there is no avoiding it so hit it head on now and educate yourself and others. There's strength in numbers and if enough say 'no' to the vaccine there won't be much they can do about it.

And now they are going after the money, bills and coins, saying the virus can live for days or longer on it scaring people into thinking cash is bad.

Don't worry, everyone will have a Federal Reserve wallet being issued to them in 2021 and the Fed is going to begin issuing 'digital currency'…not that that's all it's been doing since its inception in 1913 creating our money out of thin air!!

Look into SB3571, the Banking for All Act, because that also is coming right up and has legislation related to your upcoming personal Federal Reserve Wallet.

This will tie into something coming called 'The Great Reset', which is the collapse of the global economy and replacing the entire global economy and causing our lives to revolve around the green agenda/religion I talked about in my first book.

This will be probably be facilitated using the Rockefeller Foundation's 'Operation Lockstep', another item you need to immediately familiarize yourself with while you can…and take notes…and tell others.

In a nutshell, the current pandemic is supposed to go all the way to March of 2025. This will absolutely destroy the global economy, which is exactly what they want. This timeline is also confirmed by the World Bank, they aren't hiding anything.

Operation Lockstep was officially called "Scenarios for the Future of Technology and International Development" by the Rockefeller Foundation …."under the guise of a pandemic, we will create a prison state"

We're well on our way…

I know I just mentioned it, but I want to expand slightly on what is being called 'The Great Reset'. It's pretty important, I think it's on the cover of Time magazine this month…

"A global plan called the Great Reset is underway. Its architect is a global elite that wants to subdue all humanity, imposing coercive _**measures with which to drastically limit individual freedoms, and those of entire populations."**_

-Archbishop Carlo Maria Vigano

Remember the World Economic Forum from an earlier update? I was going to tell you about this but I'll just drop the address for the link and they can tell you themselves what they have in store for us:

https://www.weforum.org/great-reset/

It looks like the 'pandemic' is going to get really bad, whether they release a mutated virus and it actually does, or if they just use the media to convince everyone it is bad enough to shut down the world and crash the economies into dust.

The reason Congress has had no problem doling out trillions of dollars in COVID-19 relief is because soon it's not going to matter how much we owe, it will all be wiped clean...along with all our savings, our jobs and everything else...a true 'reset'....for all, and I mean ALL. When it all goes down you will only have what you possess physically so if you have money in the bank you better be turning it into lead real quick.

Everything is in place to set this off. They have about all the world's gold squirreled away. They have their private underground bunkers. Jimmy Carter put all the FEMA legislation in place to 'legally' suspend the Constitution and bring in tyrannical martial law. Vaccine Injury Law put in place in 1986. They own and control the media with even FOX news now having jumped ship (use Newsmax or OANN for now).

All media/Hollywood/celebrities/Universities/tax-free Foundations/ public school teachers are largely or entirely on the 'left', which is now 100% completely aligned with the Great Plan agenda of open borders, forced vaccinations, socialism and abortions for all up to day of birth.

The global government is in place (United Nations), it just needs to be empowered which won't happen until the USA bites the dust...if Biden gets in, we are done. Even with Trump in we've already smashed our ship upon the rocks via the plannedemic. Can Trump fix the hull and bail us out? I hope so, but my hope is small.

On a final note, Project Veritas is great to keep track of, a true outlet for legit whistleblowers, etc. If you have extra time, look into all the old email dumps from Wikileaks about 'pizzagate' in particular, what was in the emails, and who is involved. Pizzagate was to the left what 'Boystown' was to the right in the 1980s…something else to look up. You already know both sides are dirty.

Lastly, ammo prices are going through the roof. 9 mm rounds are now a buck a piece…. wow. That, to me, is not a good 'sign of the times'.

So this is farewell for now, friend, I'm already working on the next chapter for book 3 and of course a new update. It won't be out before the end of the year so I'll talk to you in 2021…I pray. Please make as best preparations as you can on all fronts, who knows what tomorrow will bring.

Oh yeah, there is something else attributed to Sir Isaac Newton I wanted to bring to your attention, a quote:

"About the times of the End, a body of men will be raised up who will turn their attention to the prophecies, and insist upon their literal interpretation, in the midst of much clamor and opposition."

Thanks for your ongoing support, I sure appreciate you passing on that my works are in existence for those that have eyes to see and ears to hear. I'm just a self-published, part-time author but if my books ever went viral, I will get right out of construction and on this endeavor full time!! Please pray that I'm able to pull this off, I want to get in there and fight for you…and Yah.

"Who will stand up for Me against evildoers? Who will take his stand for Me against those who do wickedness?"
-Psalm 94:16

Yah's blessing to you and yours, your friends and family, all your loved ones…you all will surely need it heading into 2021.

-Sentinel Jeff Hays

RISE OF THE NEW WORLD ORDER: BOOK SERIES UPDATE AND URGENT STATUS REPORT VOL. 5

APRIL 15, 2021

Table of Contents

<u>NWO...Comin' in HOT:</u>

The following is from my first book, <u>Rise of the New World Order:</u> <u>The Culling of Man</u>, Chapter 12/C: *"What Do We Do"*, published January 2013:

"Now, the points I just listed are only the most important. Everything else in this book should also be further researched by you, my newly-awakened friend. Don't take my word for anything I've said as the gospel truth. Turn off your TV. Shut off the video games. Put down your handheld devices, and get on the computer and start researching this stuff. Knowledge is power, and you have been denied the real knowledge of what is going on. You have been denied the power you and the rest of humanity deserve. This is why the world is such a messed-up place today. <u>The time to research the contents of this book is short, so I highly suggest you get on it.</u>

If you truly understand what is in this book, you should feel just like I did when I found out about it: like you just got kicked in the stomach.

The last thing you should try to feel, and this is what the proponents of the Great Plan are counting on, is to be paralyzed with fear. You've still got to live your life. You've still got to go to work. You've still got a family to raise and look after. And now you've got some "homework" and that is how you should look at the sum total of this book as: <u>an outline of subjects you need to look into.</u>

I want you to pick yourself up, dust yourself off, and educate yourself while you can, <u>because this type of information is soon to be outlawed as "inciting or promoting domestic terrorism".</u>

That feeling in your stomach will go away, trust me. Let it be replaced with what you should be feeling over finding out about the Great Plan: Anger, and the motivation to do something about it in the name of your family, your country, and hopefully your God.

Remember the quote from the start of this book:

"The world is a dangerous place to live; not because of the people who are evil, but because of the people who don't do anything about it."
-Albert Einstein

→*Our first and second amendment rights are soon to be on the chopping block, as the 4th amendment already has and others, under the ever-growing threat of "domestic terrorism" i.e., PEOPLE WAKING UP TO THE TRUTH OF THE GREAT PLAN AND WANTING TO DO SOMETHING ABOUT IT.*

"How fortunate for the leaders that the masses do not think."
–Adolph Hitler, one of the greatest leaders of the Great Plan

Sooner or later good and decent men and women are going to have to draw a line in the sand and stand unflinchingly behind it or they are going to steamroll right over free humanity and it will all be over.

Unfortunately for you and me, this is an impossibility at this time because most people are "asleep". Hopefully at this point in this book you are now "awake", and I highly recommend you go back and re-read this book at least one more time, if not more, to better understand what the tangled, interconnected web of the New World Order really is.

The time to act is now or never because it will be too late for you to educate yourself and others if you procrastinate.

The most effective thing you can do to fight back against the New World Order is to educate others as to what is going on that they are not told about---or intentionally mislead about--- by the Mainstream Media.

I love my country, the United States of America, and I will not stand idly by and watch as she is ravaged in a gang-rape by the proponents of the New World Order.

The people who are running our country are purposefully attempting to take her down and be absorbed into a one world government. I couldn't stand idly by knowing this is going on if my life depended on it, it's just not in me.

There was an old typing class exercise in school that you may or may have not come across in your life, but it is worth bringing up here:

"Now is the time for all good men to come to the aid of your country."

That time is NOW…. or *never*. We are at the threshold of the totalitarian one world government, and if we allow the United States to fall, our lives will all change for the worse. Much, much worse.

Are you going to be on the side of those who cause wars, mass murders, recessions, depressions, starvation, environmental catastrophes, and general malevolence, or are you going to be on the side of good, caring, moral, and decent humanity?

Even if you are not religious, you have to agree that what they have done throughout history and continue to do today would be considered "evil".

The proponents of the New World Order are nearing the goal they have been after for thousands of years: a Luciferian One World Government. They have pulled out all the stops in order to fulfill this, using their many secret and not-so-secret societies to orchestrate their master plan. They have shoved the New World Order agenda down our throats, and we've meekly accepted it after being brainwashed and co-opted by their "methods of madness".

They have control over our government, our schools, our churches, our economy, our society, and us. They literally OWN US. We have stood idly by as they have dissolved our Constitution, our morals, our values, our patriotism, and our country.

We should have stood up to them long ago and said "no", but didn't because there was no way of knowing their secretive agenda. Thanks largely to the advent of the internet, suppressed information and history has flowed forth that the Illuminati-controlled Mainstream Media could not filter or stop, so now they have to do damage control and discredit it the best they can.

Ultimately, they will outlaw transmission of this type of information, mark my words. We now know that we don't have leaders, we have mis-leaders. We have the best government corrupt money can buy, and that is who rules us.

It's time to take the reins of the country back from the robber barons and place them firmly in the hands of patriotic Americans like you and me, friend......"

Hey friend! Been a little longer than I would've liked since publishing update 4 but here we are, another update, and another downgrade to our situation I'm sorry to say.

Look at what's going on now and where we're at since I published my first book and the above passage in 2013...it's all coming true. It HAS to come true to fulfill Biblical prophecy.

With that said, I hope you understand just how bad of a spot we're in.

Once again, from the 4th update to the 5th, our current situation as citizens of the USA and humanity in general has deteriorated, and looking worse going forward.

Our kids' future is so much darker now in terms of living a "normal" life than when I published that book in 2013, I'm ever the more certain my forecast for the whole thing coming to an end as I called in my 4th update to be what we are staring down.

The proponents of the New World Order are literally, as of the publishing date of this update, right in the middle of trying to silence the genuine, fact-based Truth Movement that I've worked so long and hard to contribute to.

The social media titans are censoring us and the truth like never before, and the puppet politicians in DC are preparing to legislate against us also in the name of "domestic terrorism"...just like I called in 2013.

They even recently co-opted the term "woke" and now BLM is using it as their slogan! Being in BLM is the exact opposite of being woke to the

NWO as BLM are factually a Marxist organization backing the destruction of the USA.

If I were to have never known the fact and truth of our reality, that we live under the thumb of King Nimrod's Babylonian Mystery Religion, I never in a million years would have had cause to believe in God, let alone get saved and claim my place in the Book of Life.

I think everyone on the planet should have the equal opportunity to know the truth if they want to, and to decide how to live their lives based on the truth and not the manufactured reality we are presented with by the proponents of the New World Order. Now THERE is some equality for you.

The Illuminati puppets in Congress are on the cusp of legislating laws against even TALKING about King Nimrod's ancient Great Plan or spreading the facts about it all in the name of 'domestic terrorism' because it's all just conspiracy theory…right? WRONG.

Now, just as I said in the last update report in November 2020, Q-anon was a false flag/psyop all along. 99% truth and 1% poison will get you in the end. The 1% being that Trump was in on the whole Q deal and to just 'trust the plan' that Trump and the military were going to take down the pedo-Satanic global cabal. Sure.

And how did that work out for the real Truth Movement?

We basically got smeared in a patently obvious false flag to those who are woke.

As a result of the Q psyop, the legit Truth Movement is now being equated with Q by the media, WHICH WAS THE _REAL_ PLAN ALL ALONG, and "Q" is being blamed for the false flag "insurrection" in DC and anything associated with what Q purports to believe in…which is largely the truth as you know.

The Q psyop put the **absolute truth** out there in order to discredit it:

**Pedo-Satanists run the world…and always have.**

This is how the world was designed, the Satanists run the planet, and I clearly show this in my first two books, The Culling of Man, and The Awakening.

Unknowing people call it 'conspiracy theory', when in fact it's Biblical prophecy unfolding before our very eyes.

The whole Q-thing was arguably an FBI-executed psyop.

The FBI doesn't work for the citizens of the USA, they work for the Illuminati as does the CIA.

The FBI is the Illuminati's private "National Police" for the USA, and are responsible for domestic operations like Q, and the CIA are the Illuminati's "International Police", responsible for stuff like overthrowing any countries who don't have a Rothschild central bank.

If you go looking it is a documented FACT that the CIA has orchestrated the overthrow of countless "dictators" in the name of democracy and then set up puppet governments with their people in charge...all to benefit the Illuminati.

Humanity has been hapless against this highly-organized, highly-funded, highly-interconnected occult group...and Satan/Azazel/El/Kronos/Saturn, and King Nimrod/the Antichrist/Baal/Moloch/Zeus/Jupiter are their two main gods.

Yes, if you're reading this for the first time, pedo-Satanists actually run the planet, but until you've done some research it's not the easiest thing to understand...especially for an atheist like I used to be!!

Keep in mind, from my first book, I was an atheist most of my life until I woke up and started researching the New World Order.

Only two years into my research and I was 'born again' in early 2009 after waking up to the NWO in 2007.

Hallelu-Yah.

The people who run the planet today and always have **used to do their sick, occult Satanic blood rituals in public back in the day and it**

was accepted as the norm! This is factual ancient history, and once you understand that Satan and King Nimrod were passed around nearly every ancient religion and mythology in different incarnations but always the same pecking order with Satan #1, you will REALLY get an understanding of ancient history.

Again, this is all in my first two books with factual examples of everything to do with showing who really rules the world….and always have.

Remember? This is the very beginning for my first book's description on Amazon since 2013:

"The same occult group who have been ruling over humanity for thousands of years continue to do so to this day. The Luciferian one world government of Biblical prophecy is unfolding behind the scenes as you read this, and was given the catchy name of the New World Order…"

The Bible tells us multiple times that Satan is the 'god of this world'.

This means whoever worships him gets to rule the world as his underlings.

It has ALWAYS been this way if you look into it, and it will be this way to the End, culminating with the Antichrist himself running the world for Satan.

Perfect.

So, let's see what has happened since I put out the last update #4…oh yes, the election outcome. That was painful to watch unfold but I'm not one bit surprised at the outcome.

Let's go once more to what I was talking about with regards to elections in my first book back in 2013…

From "Rise of the New World Order: The Culling of Man", chapter 7/A, "Voting Machine Fraud", released January 2013:

Let's start off with the people who we "elected" to drive our country straight into the ground….

Campaign donations and clandestine actions from pro-New World Order entities aside, we've got a terrible issue we need to address, and that is a legitimate, factual concern about voting machine fraud.

The proponents of the Great Plan have pulled out all the stops to advance their agenda, and have left no avenue uncompromised to complete their mission.

Think about this: The 50 states in the USA are divided into over 3,000 counties. Ohio, for instance, is divided into 88 counties, Iowa is divided into 99 counties, and so on. In approximately 1% of these counties, there are paper ballots which are hand counted properly, the way all of our counties should be counting our ballots. This respectable 1% consists of about half of the counties in New Hampshire---the "Live Free or Die" state---and a very few, very small counties scattered throughout the rest of the United States.

In 99% of the other compromised counties, the Democratic and Republican controlled Boards of Elections make sure that the ballots are commandeered from the neighborhood precincts as the polls close their doors. This is to make sure that the neighborhood citizens and other watchdog-patriots do NOT have a chance to count, or at least spot-check, their own votes.

Such counting or spot-checking by the citizens would make centralized computer vote-rigging impossible. This is why the Illuminati, who today control both the national Democratic and Republican parties through the CFR, vehemently oppose any such citizen participation at the neighborhood precinct level. This is because centralized counting is the common feature of all governments trying to rig elections.

"Those who cast the votes decide nothing. Those who count the votes decide everything."
-Joseph Stalin, alleged 33rd degree Freemason, candidly speaking the truth

In these 99% of USA counties, citizens are forced to use either computer or machine methods of casting a ballot. Vote counting is wide open for fraud this way. The Democratic and Republican parties at the county level delegate the "counting" to one of a small handful of privately-owned companies which count 99% of the votes in United States national elections in complete secret, with no independent verification or audit.

Currently the four companies which are delegated the power to count the votes in the USA were Election Systems & Software, Diebold, Hart, and Sequoia.

The local county election boards use armed guards to make sure the citizens, candidates, and reporters cannot see what these private companies are doing to the ballots in the "counting room" on election night.

Since 1973, the powers behind the RNC and the DNC have arm-twisted, persuaded, and bullied the local governments in most counties in the USA to unconstitutionally delegate the vote counting to these four mysterious companies. By 1988, the counting companies had consolidated their control over 49 states, and half of New Hampshire.

The private companies controlling the ballots are given a direct feed to a team of manipulators which represent a pool of the AP wire service and the major TV Networks, all under Illuminati control.

The vote-fraud cartel was further empowered through the implementation of the criminal "Help Americans Vote Act" of 2002 or HAVA, which should really be called the "Helping the New World Order by Computer Fraud" Act.

HAVA appropriated $4 billion of our money to entice the state and county election offices to implement computer "vote-counting" systems from basically three major companies, Diebold, Sequoia, and Election Systems & Software. These systems provide for no paper trail and no citizen checks and balances. Most people have no idea how their vote is counted, and I'm here to tell you as of right now under this system, your vote doesn't count.

The patriotic organization "Citizens for a Fair Vote Count" has estimated that it would take no more than $400 million dollars per election to hand count every vote on every ballot in the United States. Because the New World Order proponents and their Mainstream Media insist on easily rigged elections, all you hear is how we can't possibly afford the expense of a hand count.

We spend hundreds of BILLIONS of dollars supporting out world military empire. Billions of dollars were just spent on just the promotion and advertising for the 2012 Presidential election alone. Why would billions of dollars be spent for a job that only pays $400,000 year unless someone else besides the President is going to benefit? You already know the answer to that.

We can easily fund an honest and accountable vote-counting system by the people, for the people; to ensure that who we want running the country is who gets into power. This is the only way we are going to get our foot in the door and get some real "change" in this country.

So, in a nutshell, it's either paper ballots/hand counting for an honest election and real change, or corrupted centralized computer counting by the proponents of the New World Order and the usual suspects stay in office...over and over and over, pushing our country further and further under water.

Which would you prefer?

Well, here we are. Trump and the Patriotic American People weren't nearly as powerful as the Illuminati and their underlings. Not even close, and that shouldn't surprise you. The Presidency was literally handed right to Biden.

I don't know what to make of all the Sidney Powell/Linn Wood statements. Where is the "Kraken"? And not a thing Linn Wood said was going to happen did. It was a complete S-show from the get-go!

There sure appeared to be voter fraud. If you have not seen Mike Lindell's video about it, I highly suggest you do, but it seems no one is powerful enough, even a sitting President, to even have the facts broadcast in public because the canned mainstream and social media is covering for the NWO-Biden Presidency.

So where are we now with Trump? Don't feel too bad because Trump could have done way better for us and no matter who is in there the Great Plan marches on.

Did Trump try to eliminate the Federal Reserve? Nope.

Was there a new 9/11 investigation by a truly independent agency. No.

Anything become of the Hunter Biden laptop? Negative.

Was Hillary arrested? Ha!

Did Trump re-authorize the traitorous NDAA against us? Yes, he did.

Did Trump push hazardous, experimental vaccines with no long-term studies on an unsuspecting public in the name of saving the economy and his reputation? That's a BIG yes there....ugh.

The fact is that the number one thing Trump could have done to MAGA would have been to eliminate the Federal Reserve and take the money power back from the Illuminati and back in the hands of the Congress as it dictates in the Constitution.

Article 1, Section 8, Clause 5 of the United States Constitution:

[The Congress shall have Power . . .] To coin Money, regulate the Value thereof, and of foreign Coin, and fix the Standard of Weights and Measures; ...

Trump surely did do some good stuff for our country. He pulled us out of the treasonous TPP.... which Biden just put us back in via Executive Order.

Trump pulled us out of the diabolical Paris Climate Accord, which will financially strangle the United States and Europe under regulations and lets China and India get away with climate murder. Biden just signed us back up with an Executive Order.

All those Executive Orders aren't coming from Biden, they are coming from his bosses over at the CFR, and the CFR gets their marching orders from the owners of the privately-owned, for-profit corporation you know as the Federal Reserve.

Pretty much every EO that Biden has put out there is detrimental to the United States...which is us: you and me and our families and friends.

With Trump largely out of the picture, mainstream media will now, instead of bashing Trump 24/7, switch over to full-out pushing the NWO-agenda with Climate Change at the top of the agenda.

The political left has literally morphed into the party of the New World Order and will remain so until the End.

In the 1960s the left was all anti-government, anti-censorship, anti-war, full of hippie-love for their fellow man, etc. Now they are exactly the polar opposite of all that. Just shows how controlled the whole thing is and how powerful the media is as it steers our boat towards full-on one world government. The one world government of the End is in place, it's the United Nations. It just needs to be empowered which will happen after the USA crashes and burns coming right up.

Now that Biden/Harris have been put into position to fully take us down that road to full-blown New World Order tyranny, they have some time to make up.

For all the talk about Trump being a dictatorial fascist, then what is Biden?

He's already signed more Executive Orders faster to circumvent Congress than any other President in history to "correct" the damage Trump did to the Great Plan.

Biden just signed into law on 3/11/21 The American Rescue Plan Act of 2021. Another couple trillion dollars of insider payoffs and pork thrown on the multi-trillion-dollar life-support system for a dying United States.

Remember when we all got a few hundred dollars each in stimulus checks in 2008 to help fight off the Great Recession? My family has received thousands of dollars in stimulus money at this point....easily 10x the amount in 2008. Does that mean things are 10x worse with this new recession? I'd say about 100x worse, but that won't be apparent to the general public until it is too late. But we know what's up, right? Right.

Why would they call it a 'rescue plan' if the economy wasn't gut-shot like I've been saying. The stock market might seem to be flying high but it is easily manipulated and due to its effect on public sentiment, people think the economy is doing fine when it's all a smoke screen.

In early April 2021 in just one week over 700,000 _new_ unemployment claims were filed...that's not good at all!

But, hey, everybody's getting another check. Everyone is getting vaccinated and everything is slowly getting back to 'normal'...geeez. Biden was talking about the next stimulus before the ink was even dry on the current 'rescue' stimulus!

On one hand you've got a high-flying stock market and rich people are getting richer, and on the other hand you've got the Federal Government with a giant fire hose that sprays money trying to put out the fire burning ever-larger within the U.S. economy as a result of all the shutdowns. Throw in Biden's EO's eliminating those pipeline jobs and cutting our economic throat via the Paris Climate Accord, TPP, bringing in illegals, etc.

They don't care about running the National Debt up to the Moon because you know how you get rid of the debt? A dollar crisis and then martial law.

You cannot print trillions of dollars out of thin air without repercussions.

Hyperinflation is beginning right now and has been ramping up for years.

Notice how the portions of processed food in the grocery stores has been going down while prices have been inching up at the same time?

Seen lumber prices lately? Or real estate? Or silver and gold? And look at Bitcoin go. These are the canaries in the coal mine we need to be paying attention to.

The Federal Reserve stated that they are leaving interest rates where they are, at ZERO, until the end of 2023. If the Fed announces an emergency meeting to discuss, address and act upon the hyperinflation fuse that has been lit, you can expect a historic selloff on Wall Street, which should be enough to set the other dominoes in motion like the housing bubble, the derivatives bubble, and everything else that went off to cause the Great Recession of 2008.

The big difference is that the Fed doesn't have any more ammo in terms of being able to lower interest rates to stimulate the economy. They are already at zero. They are just flat-out throwing monopoly money at us now.

They've been planning this for years, put the legislation for FEMA/ Martial Law into place under Jimmy Carter, have built their own personal underground survival shelters...and are ready to light the fuse on the Great Reset.

The Great Reset and the plannedemic are related, planned and executed by the same people...as ~~usual~~ *always*.

As for the current state of the plannedemic?

The seasonal flu and cold season mysteriously disappeared in 2020... lowest levels seen ever.

That's not possible.

People aren't getting the flu *and* covid in one season, they are getting the flu and it's showing up as Covid 19. Same with the common cold!

According to Webmd(dot)com 'coronavirus' variants are responsible for 20% of the annual cold season. Those cases are surely showing up as coronavirus because they are!

From what I've read and understood, any virus can be shown to be 'covid19' if they run enough cycles on the PCR test. In fact, the WHO just came out a few weeks ago and instructed testers to turn down the number of cycles because they were just now concerned about false positives...what a load of crap! All of last year they were running too many cycles and people with no symptoms were testing positive for coronavirus.

Not only were people that weren't sick or had a virus other than covid 19 testing positive for covid 19, some people suspicious of what was going on had non-human items tested and they were turning up positive for covid 19 too!

The President of Tanzania went public that he had results of PCR tests showing that a sample from a goat, a papaya, and a paw paw tree all tested positive for covid 19.

Now that Trump is out and Biden is in, the newly-altered PCR tests will result in the covid19 diagnosis to drop to 'show' that the vaccines and ridiculous mask-mandates are working.

Remember, this false flag plannedemic was never about us dealing with a random, naturally-occurring virus. It was about introducing a bioweapon and stampeding the sheeple into the vaccine that I guarantee you they've had ready to go for a long time...and they know the long-term results.

In fact, it seems there are no end of "issues" going on with Johnson and Johnson's and AstraZeneca's vaccines, which don't use the mRNA technology...issues that are pushing people more and more over to seeking out the mRNA vaxxes from Moderna and Pfizer.

Just a few days ago it was announced that 15 million doses of JnJ's vaccine had to be destroyed due to a manufacturing error. And they had said that AstraZeneca's vaccine was causing blood clots and scared everyone and on 4/13/21 the US federal government suspended JnJ's vaccine domestically because of only 6 people out of 7 millions shots administered had cause the same blood clot issue.

If you look up the VAERS data through the CDC you can factually see that the mRNA vaccines have killed thousands of people by this point, but the CDC doesn't have a problem with that??? Unbelievable. You KNOW that something is just not right by just that fact alone.

It's not to hard to take a look into the future to see what the long-term health effects will be from taking the mRNA "vaccine". This particular "vaccine" is no such thing, in reality it's gene therapy. Just because it comes in a syringe and is injected with a needle doesn't make it a vaccine. It is a DNA-altering technology with no published long-term effects of turning your immune system against itself.

This mRNA technology injection teaches your body how to make a protein-marker allegedly from the covid 19 virus. Not the virus itself, but a part of the virus, so in that way it is similar to a traditional vaccine.

The big difference is that a traditional vaccine only puts a set amount of viral material for your body's immune system to target.

The mRNA gene therapy teaches your immune system to **create** and then **attack** the covid 19 protein that your own body's cells are now making.

Forever.

So, your body's immune system is always jacked up because there is always a marker being manufactured within the body that the immune system has to fight. Forever.

This is the exact definition of autoimmune disease. The mRNA literally introduces autoimmune disease into your body. What a wonderful idea...not.

Long-term side effects will not be known to the public for months and years, and if it turns out the mRNA vaccine side-effects were a *"an unforeseen and unfortunate occurrence"* then it will be too late.

I believe the long-term side effects will turn up mainly as one particular disease, I don't know what yet...but we will. And it will have a name.

And of course, now they are saying there are **many different mutations of covid 19**...this is impossible, but we sure called that one from update 1 didn't we, friend?

Remember the words of that one reputable virologist from my first update when this whole 'pandemic' deal was getting off the ground Winter/Spring 2020? He said Covid 19 is an engineered virus...it can't mutate because it's not natural, and it will certainly fizzle out as it's an unstable, man-made virus.

This is why they keep releasing "variants" all over the world to keep this thing going.

There is a Great Britain variant. And a Brazillian. And a South African. And blah blah blah the sky is falling. And of course, there's one for the USA to try and terrorize and stampede everyone into the mRNA vaccines.

As of right now, they are saying the new strains are twice as contagious so watch out! Go get your vaccine before it's too late and you kill someone's grandma!! Although there is a 99.6% chance of surviving hurry out and get your experimental vaccine that has zero liability for the manufacturers!!

They haven't said yet if there are more deadly strains to come, but I'm sure that's coming to scare those who are "vaccine hesitant" into taking the mRNA vaccines.

So, what's going to happen if they give 90% of the planet the mRNA vaccine? Ever heard of the Culling of Man? Ever heard of the Georgia Guidestones calling for only 500,000,000 or fewer people to be allowed to live at one time?

Maybe I should get the mRNA vaccine because I don't know if I want to be around at that point....Just kidding!! I've still got a lot of fight left in me lol. But I will not be getting this vaccine, no way, no how.

And how about this clown Fauci. First, he said don't bother masking up. Then it was mask up. Now in January 2021 it's TWO masks.

Are they going to close everything down again because the flu is coming next year? They never should have shut down to start with. The government should have advised people to stay home but told them of the risks.

Remember the images coming out of China at the start of 2020 with dead bodies in the streets and first-responders in full-body hazmat suits???

If YOU want to stay home and cower go ahead, but the stores never should have been shut down.

The proponents of the Great Plan for Global Enslavement are behind on their timetable to prepare for the appearance of the Antichrist, and this is necessitating a Great Reset to put their Train of Tyranny back on the tracks and full speed ahead.

The Great Reset:

You may have heard about the **"Great Reset"**, but what is it?

The so-called Great Reset promises to bring about *"a more secure, more equal, and more stable world"* if everyone on the planet agrees to *"act jointly and swiftly to revamp all aspects of our societies and economies, from education to social contracts and working conditions."*

The above quotations come from Klaus Schwab, founder and head of the World Economic Forum, on November 17, 2020. This is only 5 months or so ago at this point.

Allow me to translate from NWO-speak to what Schwab's words **REALLY** mean to you and me: *"The Great Reset promises a global police state, with global socialism for all after the ultimate economic crash of all time and subsequent starvation from the pandemonium, giving way to what's left of humanity alive that didn't starve or die from the mRNA vaccines surrendering their lives and will to the UN as the new, all-powerful global government"*

Since symbols and words (**SPELL**-ing) are **SO** important to the pedo-Satanic occultists running the **_Great Plan_**, let's start with the word 'reset' to see what is on the NWO agenda for the world.

Merriam-Webster defines 'reset', when used in vocabulary, as a *transitive verb.* This means that it is an 'action'.

But what action?

Calling a reset 'great' signifies high importance, or high impact, or big in scale.

Ok. So, what is this high-importance, high-impact action?

It's the intentional global financial crash to destroy the 'concept' of capitalism, and to **_reset_** us all into the one world government (United Nations) and global **_socialism_**.

This is why the public schools, particularly lately in the USA, have been pushing extreme leftism and socialism as trendy and cool.

And it worked.

We now have two generations in the USA, Millennials/Gen Y and Gen Z, who have been brainwashed to be pro-NWO.

As the next generation comes to voting age, which someone decided to call "Generation Alpha", this mindset is going to start showing up at the polls and voting for the NWO agenda overwhelmingly and this will legitimately put the majority of the people behind it to back the coming tyranny!!!

It's going to be Nazi Germany all over again on steroids and the Antichrist starring as Hitler. Not a pretty picture, but it is coming plain as day.

I would define the word "reset" in the context they are using it as "to intentionally undo something you knew wouldn't work to start with and then put it the way you wanted it all along", because that is exactly what the proponents of the New World Order are on the verge of doing.

Capitalism would work fine if the occultists weren't running it and it was truly allowed to operate independently, but they have controlled it from the start and really pirated the system in the USA with their creation of the Federal Reserve in 1913.

When the proponents of the Great Plan/NWO installed the Federal Reserve System as our nations money supply in 1913 they basically set the hourglass in motion to our country's demise. The NWO version of capitalism fails every time due to pirating the system using a privately-owned (by them) central bank.

The end result of the Federal Reserve ponzi scheme---and global fiat money ponzi scheme as the Illuminati owns and controls nearly all global central banks---is the complete destruction of the value of the dollar, which they've been chipping away at for years by inflating the money supply at will.

If you have time, I HIGHLY suggest you obtain a copy of G. Edward Griffin's classic about the Federal Reserve, money policy, and the great crash that is coming. It is called "The Creature from Jekyll Island" and it is highly reviewed and ranked.

1a. ~~Agenda 21~~ Agenda 2030

"In the event that I am reincarnated, I would like to return as a deadly virus, to contribute something to solving overpopulation."
-Prince Bernhard, 1988

You'll know from my first book, The Culling of Man, that Prince Bernhard was a co-founder of the Bilderberg Group back in 1954 with good ol' David Rockefeller. Bernhard is one of the apex members of the Illuminati. ~~I don't know if you've seen him lately but he literally looks like the Crypt Keeper...yikes!!!~~ He actually died in the middle of this update report so there you go.... good riddance.

The people running the planet are pro-population-reduction eugenicists, and the Prince was doing nothing more than being candidly truthful about how little the elite think of their slaves on the global plantation.

The new goal for the plantation, since they failed miserably to accomplish their goal by 2021 (Agenda 21), is to have everything in place by 2030, and to be ready and waiting for the Antichrist to come on the scene not long after.

The Plannedemic is the trigger, the Great Reset is the bullet and Agenda 2030 is the gun to put down the critically ailing USA.

Again, I am surely and certainly sticking to the Endtime-line I put out in Update 4 as humanity's position has yet again deteriorated since putting that out there last November 2020, *especially* in the USA.

You can expect the United Nations to feature prominently in Biden's decision-making process going forward with Agenda 2030 as the blueprint because Biden was literally installed to ram it down our throats.

One of the first Executive orders by Biden was an Executive Order which directs the USA to rejoin the Paris Climate Accord. Adhering to the PCA will contribute greatly to the downfall of our country.

Here is just the first part of this multi-page Executive Order which brought us back into the PCA:

Executive Order 14008 of January 27, 2021

Tackling the Climate Crisis at Home and Abroad

The United States and the world face a profound climate crisis. We have a narrow moment to pursue action at home and abroad in order to avoid the most catastrophic impacts of that crisis and to seize the opportunity that tackling climate change presents. Domestic action must go hand in hand with United States international leadership, aimed at significantly enhancing global action. Together, we must listen to science and meet the moment.

By the authority vested in me as President by the Constitution and the laws of the United States of America, it is hereby ordered as follows:

PART I—PUTTING THE CLIMATE CRISIS AT THE CENTER OF UNITED STATES FOREIGN POLICY AND NATIONAL SECURITY

Section 101. Policy. United States international engagement to address climate change—which has become a climate crisis—is more necessary and urgent than ever. The scientific community has made clear that the scale and speed of necessary action is greater than previously believed. There is little time left to avoid setting the world on a dangerous, potentially catastrophic, climate trajectory. Responding to the climate crisis will require both significant short-term global reductions in greenhouse gas emissions and net-zero global emissions by mid-century or before.

It is the policy of my Administration that climate considerations shall be an essential element of United States foreign policy and national security....

And this EO just goes on and on and on. Biden's Executive Orders and his entire agenda is driven by the United Nation's Agenda 2030.

Agenda 2030 is just the new branding of the continuation of the implementation of Agenda (20)21...named for the year we are in now.

Since the NWO failed to meet Agenda 21 goals they will now have their foot in the throttle since they've got the world on the ropes financially as a result of this Plannedemic.

The UN is taking a bold step towards a truly empowered one world government. They are boldly claiming that since the member nations---all controlled already by the Illuminati, including the USA---voted to authorize them to implement Agenda 2030 on the world, on every country, on every single person, that they are going to follow through without fail this time.

Agenda 2030 pledges to 'Leave No One Behind', they want all humans on Earth to have the same opportunities, jobs, healthcare, etc. They aim to do this by averaging everyone out...bringing down the 1st world countries and bringing up the 3rd world countries so everyone is the 'same'. This goes hand in hand with eliminating all borders and countries, which is the plan.

The **2030 Agenda for Sustainable Development** is a United Nations-created resolution adopted by the U.N. General Assembly in 2015. That gave them 15 years to accomplish their goals from 2015 to 2030.

They had planned on Hillary Clinton taking the reins the following year but we all know how that panned out.

Take four years out of that 15 years that Trump was in there and they are significantly behind.

Agenda 2030 dictates to humanity to execute the following by the year 2030...or else:

- End all poverty in all forms everywhere
- End hunger, achieve food security and improved nutrition and promote sustainable agriculture
- Ensure healthy lives and promote well-being for all at all ages
- Ensure inclusive and equitable quality education and promote lifelong learning opportunities for all
- Achieve gender equality and empower all women and girls

- Ensure availability and sustainable management of water and sanitation for all
- Ensure access to affordable, reliable, sustainable and modern energy for all
- Promote sustained, inclusive and sustainable economic growth, full and productive employment and decent work for all
- Build resilient infrastructure, promote inclusive and sustainable industrialization and foster innovation
- Reduce inequality within and among countries
- Make cities and human settlements inclusive, safe, resilient and sustainable
- Ensure sustainable consumption and production patterns
- Take urgent action to combat climate change and its impacts (acknowledging the United Nations Framework Convention on Climate Change)
- Conserve and sustainably use the oceans, seas and marine resources for sustainable development
- Protect, restore and promote sustainable use of terrestrial ecosystems, sustainably manage forests, combat desertification, and halt and reverse land degradation and halt biodiversity loss
- Promote peaceful and inclusive societies for sustainable development, provide access to justice for all and build effective, accountable and inclusive institutions at all levels
- Strengthen the means of implementation and revitalize the Global Partnership for Sustainable Development

With only ten years left to achieve the Sustainable Development Goals, World leaders at the SDG Summit in September 2019 called for a "Decade of Action" to implement Agenda 2030 by the target date of...2030.

In 2019 no one knew who was going to win the upcoming USA Presidential Race, and if Trump got another 4 years there was not a snowball's chance in hell of accomplishing the Illuminati's goals. Just more fuel for the fire that the election was a corrupt one.

This is just a **very brief** overview of Agenda 2030 but it is coming down the tracks like a freight train and I HIGHLY suggest you spend just a few hours and educate yourself about Agenda 2030 so you can educate those around you.

Most people nowadays are so wrapped up in the now-thousands of tee vee shows, video games, social network gossip, etc., that they are able to get away with pushing their agenda virtually unopposed except for people like you and me, friend. With everyone so distracted it's going to be much easier now to accomplish their goals for Agenda 2030.

The only thing they go to great lengths to hide is the control structure behind it and the awful truth that we are lorded over by Satan-worshippers.

In other words....we're in a bad spot!

1b. The World Economic Forum/WEF

"The pandemic represents a rare but narrow window of opportunity to reflect, reimagine and reset our world"
-Head Vampire Klaus Schwab, founder and executive chairman of the WEF, June 2020

"You'll own nothing and be happy about it"
- "Professor" Klaus Schwab, referring to the coming economic collapse that will cause humanity to embrace the fairy-tale version of UN socialism and be happy about it, and to cooperate with the Great Plan...or starve to death. November 2020

The first thing to know about Klaus is that he is not only a former attendee of the Bilderberg Group, he was a member of the Bilderberg Steering Committee so this guy is certified Illuminati elite. This is why he created and heads the WEF.

Now, we're talking about the same World Economic Forum/WEF from past updates...you know, the same one who worked with 'Slow Kill' Bill Gates on Event 201 right before the pandemic hit? Yeah, that's them, the usual suspects...as usual.

Apparently, releasing manmade bioweapons has proved to be the most effective and non-violent way to really put humanity under the globalists' collective thumb. There will be more 'pandemics' coming after Covid 19, mark my words.

I pulled this from an interview Euronews did with Schwab in November of 2020:

Interviewer: I then asked Professor Schwab how he intends to begin the reset and where he will start. He told me there are three dimensions, three priorities:

"The first one is to make the world more resilient because <u>we definitely will have to face other surprises, black swans, as they are called, maybe different kinds of viruses.</u> Second, we have to make the world more inclusive,

fairer, because we have seen that we have reached unsustainable degrees, of levels, of people who feel excluded. Finally, we have to make the world much greener. We finally have to put all our energy behind decarbonization in order to avoid a major catastrophe in the future of which we have the first signs today," Schwab added.

Let's interpret here, a 'Black Swan' is **"an unpredictable or unforeseen event, typically one with extreme consequences"**

If it's unpredictable and unforeseen, how in the HELL does Schwab know that **"we definitely will have to face other surprises, black swans, as they are called, MAYBE DIFFERENT KINDS OF VIRUSES".**

It is also possible, even probable IMHO, he is referring to the "unforeseen" long-term effects of the mRNA "vaccines" from Moderna and Pfizer.

He knows events are coming, and *what* events, because he's a card-carrying member of the Illuminati and he is telling us bad things are going to happen and soon, knowing the sheep are too dumbed-down and distracted to be able to pick up on what he's saying, but his cohorts in the know all are able to hear loud and clear what is coming.

The rest of Klaus' above statement from the interview has to do with pushing Agenda 2030 and the 'green religion' that people are slowly being indoctrinated to.

It seems that Klaus and the WEF are taking the lead from NWO stalwarts like Bilderberg and putting the Great Plan agenda right out in the open and no one is paying attention.

The WEF, founded in 1971 by Schwab, is basically the new Bilderberg Group. Their annual meeting began in 1974 and is simply called 'Davos' because that is where it happens, in Davos, Switzerland.

Davos is the same concept as Bilderberg, hundreds of elites getting together semi-secretly to decide what direction to take humanity, world democracies be damned.

Schwab is the front man at the least, and at most the architect of the Great Reset, as it is being directed from the WEF control room.

Schwab even put their diabolical plans into a book and it's on Amazon... being dragged mercilessly by those who are awake in the comments.

First, here is the book description from Amazon for Schwab's '**COVID-19:The Great Reset**', published July 9, 2020:

"**COVID-19: The Great Reset**" is a guide for anyone who wants to understand how COVID-19 disrupted our social and economic systems, *and what changes will be needed to create a more inclusive, resilient and sustainable world going forward.* Klaus Schwab, founder and executive Chairman of the World Economic Forum, and Thierry Malleret, founder of the Monthly Barometer, explore what the root causes of these crisis were, and why they lead to a need for a Great Reset. Theirs is a worrying, yet hopeful analysis. COVID-19 has created a great disruptive reset of our global social, economic, and political systems. But the power of human beings lies in being foresighted and having the ingenuity, at least to a certain extent, to take their destiny into their hands and to plan for a better future. This is the purpose of this book: to shake up and to show the deficiencies which were manifest in our global system, even before COVID broke out."

So, you mean to tell me that in under 6 months of 'pandemic', not even knowing how allegedly serious it was going to be until well into 2020, that Schwab was able to tie leveraging the 'pandemic' to fulfill the goals of Agenda 2030 and put it all in a book, edit it, and publish on July 9, 2020???

Not buying it...not one iota. This book was probably written 2-5 years ago.

A ton of awake people have piled on in the comments section for this book, calling him and the NWO agenda to the carpet, here is just one review of many, the 'most helpful' ranked by readers, and this guy is AWAKE!!!:

Rated book 1 out of 5 stars *"The Call for 'Global Governance' is Chilling"*
Reviewed in the United States on September 1, 2020

The book not only calls for 'global governance', but also for a heightened cooperation between the 'private sector' and the 'public sector'.

Private sector: banks and corporations (private interests)

Public sector: the government (public welfare)

The fact that you're trying to involve private interests in the conversation about public welfare is hilarious. Americans want a government that represents the People, not a handful of oligarchs who rig the system to benefit themselves. America will be the greatest threat to the 'Great Reset' for this reason.

In fact, saying that 'capitalism is broken' is pretty disingenuous when you consider that banks and corporations are the ones who broke it in the first place.

Aren't we only 12 years removed from the 2008 financial crisis? And you think the people of America trust you to install 'global governance'? After our institutions have proved to be unworthy of our trust . . ?

Private sector influence in the public sector is what caused our economic woes to begin with. I seriously doubt giving banks and corporations MORE of a role in government is going to benefit us in any way. I have a radical idea: let's get money OUT of politics, not invite more of it IN.

I realize that most people don't have any economic sensibility whatsoever, but I think the WEF is underestimating the number of people who are raising eyebrows at this whole 'Great Reset' thing. Perhaps that's why radical revolutions so frequently entail locking up the educated. If you're somewhat intelligent, you see right through the lie. And so into the gulag you go! (Hopefully they have pizza in 21st century concentration camps. I need pizza.)

All in all, I was not impressed with the book. I've been paying attention to the UN's Agenda 21/2030 for awhile, but I always thought they'd pull it off a lot more smoothly than they are. As it stands right now, a lot of people are viewing this as a plot to subvert American democracy. The question is: Why isn't this big news?

-S. Lawrence

1,833 people found this helpful

The WEF actually just had the Davos 2021 meeting! It was from January 25-29, 2021.

Here is a statement from the Davos 2021 homepage:

Davos Agenda:

"The COVID-19 pandemic has demonstrated that no institution or individual alone can address the economic, environmental, social and technological challenges of our complex, interdependent world. The pandemic has accelerated systemic changes that were apparent before its inception. The fault lines that emerged in 2020 now appear as critical crossroads in 2021. The time to rebuild trust and to make crucial choices is fast approaching as the need to reset priorities and the urgency to reform systems grow stronger around the world."

Obviously, there is a ton more information about the WEF, Davos meetings, and Darth Schwab, but that is on you. We've got to keep moving here...

1C. The Great Reset Goes Off

There are many scenarios I can envision to bring humanity to its knees and ultimately beg for the United Nations to save them instead of the good ol' reliable, money-is-no-object USA...and that is the end goal: Every person and every aspect of human existence on planet Earth is to be under the authority of the United Nations, including what's left of the USA.

The United Nations will decide what your occupation will be, whether you get to eat, or even if you get to live...just like the old Soviet Union.

The scenario I'm betting on is complete global economic collapse brought on by the after-effects of the plannedemic.

We're still a gut-shot deer wandering through the woods on adrenaline and the NWO keeps giving us more blood in the form of trillions of dollars of fiat monopoly money...this won't work for much longer as you simply can't print your way out of a collapse that's been coming for decades now.

Hyperinflation appears to be setting in right now and if the Federal Reserve calls an emergency meeting to address this you can expect the stock markets to instantly tank.

As a side note, I'm expecting mass casualties in 2-3 years from everyone who got the mRNA vaccine, so if they vaccinate/exterminate 60-70% of everyone alive today that will take the global population down nicely...which would also collapse the economy if it hasn't died by then from hyperinflation.

Billions of people suddenly coming down with terminal cancer or God-knows-what-else from the long-term mRNA effects of activating your immune system to attack the host and not being able to turn it off would not only overwhelm the hospitals it would completely destroy the world economy. That many deaths would annihilate the global supply chain and we would be on our own in a zombie apocalypse.

So, for the Illuminati, it comes down to basic math:

On 4/5/21 Schwab, some elected world leaders like Angela Merkel and Boris Johnson, and others went on record to state that "unvaccinated people are a threat to humanity" and that "the 'Great Reset' needs to include the establishment of a global "pandemic" treaty. It certainly was never about the pandemic but to get everyone to take the mRNA vaccines to cull them.

Less people on the planet alive = less people to keep track of and control... and resist them.

We talked about this in my first book, but another ticking time bomb that could kick off the Great Reset is a derivatives implosion. Hedge funds, which utilize legalized corruption and stealing to manipulate the stock market and skim off profits left and right, are behaving more and more reckless all the time. You can thank Bubba Clinton for eliminating the Glass-Steagall Act for this one and again this is all in my first book.

There is another housing bubble ripe for the bursting right this second... Remember 2008?

With so many time bombs sitting around waiting to go off and all interconnected, when one goes, they all go and this is why this crash will be the worst in mankind's history.

And also figure this in: With Biden at the helm and the NWO in full control, tensions in the Middle East have skyrocketed and Iran could easily be scapegoated in an EMP false flag against the United States, or even North Korea for that matter as leader Kim is also rattling his sabre also against Biden as of late.

In early January of 2021, just days before Biden took office, North Korean leader Kim Jong Un called for more advanced nuclear weapons and said the United States is "our biggest enemy."

That's a far cry from where we were with Trump at the helm, walking ALONE into North Korea to meet with Kim so it's going to get crazy under Biden.

Our interconnected, electrical, digital structured world will also be our undoing because when one part breaks the whole machine goes down.

This was recently evidenced by what happened in just Texas. Imagine if the whole grid went down...I believe it will someday.

They know this is coming so on one front the elites have built hundreds of private, deep underground bunkers that the public can't find or even get into. Also, many have access to the military DUMBs, that's Deep Underground Military Bases, to survive a societal breakdown. They didn't spend trillions building this stuff because they WEREN'T planning on using them!

On the other front, the elites have enacted legislation, including the establishment of FEMA under Jimmy Carter, to deal with the slaves after a breakdown. They aren't going to all of this trouble putting this legislation in place decades before they need it because things are going to be just fine, you've got to read the tea leaves, which is what we're doing.

So. The economy crashes, the grid crashes as a result, and society breaks down into survival elements.

Once people reach the starvation stage, which won't take long, they will do anything for food, including capitulating to the UN's demands that they are now in charge.... if you want to eat and live.

I said it before and I'll say it again: it only took that Peruvian rugby team that crashed in the Andes in the early 1970s <u>nine days without food</u> before they were so desperate with hunger they resorted to eating the dead bodies of their friends to survive.

This is even evidenced in the animal world where animals will fight to the death over food as opposed to water because food is much harder to come by.

It is this basic need to eat---at all costs--- that the Illuminati will use against humanity to help fulfill Agenda 2030 after the financial crash.

"Control oil and you control nations; control food and you control the people"

And also:

"Who controls the food supply, controls the people..."

-Card-carrying Illuminati Henry Kissinger, issuing both of these quotes in the early 1970s

He's right of course, as they always are.

I see as of mid-January of this year, 2021, Bill Gates has taken some of his fiat monopoly money and bought up enough of America's farmlands to become the largest farmland owner in the United States.

That's because he knows what's coming, what I'm trying to show you right now.

Whatever you hold physically in your hand will be all you're worth coming right up. All of Gates' billions in the stock market will vanish and only what he holds in physical assets will be worth anything in the near future.

With what's coming, food will the most valuable commodity of all and Gates knows this!! What a scumbag. Would love to see him sporting a Columbian Necktie about now...

The new wealth after the crash will be food and the means of producing it just to keep humanity going, otherwise the Illuminati will have no slaves at all. No slaves = no power.

There are bad times coming, I shouldn't have to tell you this at this point.

The craziness of the year 2020 is going to just keep rolling... all... decade... long.

The Great Reset. Prepare yourselves because it's coming.

Conclusion

This quote is from Update 2/May 2020 and is worth repeating as Kennedy is vastly more knowledgeable than I am (for right now!) when it comes to vaccines interacting with the human biological system:

"Pharma has 80 COVID vaccines in development, but Gates & Fauci pushed Moderna's "Frankenstein jab" to the front of the line.

Scientists & ethicists are sounding alarms...

The vaccine uses a new, untested, and very controversial experimental mRNA technology that Gates has backed for over a decade.

Instead of injecting an antigen & adjuvant as with traditional vaccines, Moderna plugs a small piece of coronavirus genetic code into human cells, altering DNA throughout the human body and reprograming our cells to produce antibodies to fight the virus.

MRNA vaccines are a form of genetic engineering called "germ line gene editing". <u>Moderna's genetic alterations are passed down to future generations.</u>

In January, The Geneva Statement (the world's leading ethicists and scientists) called for an end to this kind of experimentation.

Moderna has never brought a product to market, proceeded through clinical trials, or had a vaccine approved by FDA.

Despite Gates' investments, the company, was teetering on bankruptcy with $1.5 billion debt before COVID.

Fauci's support won the company an astonishing $483 million in federal funds to accelerate development.

Dr. Joseph Bolen, <u>Moderna's former R&D Chief</u>, expressed shock at Fauci's bet. "I don't know what their thinking was", he told CNN, "When I read that, I was pretty amazed".

Moderna and Fauci launched federally-funded human trials on March 3rd, 2020 in Seattle.

Dr. Peter Hotez warns of potentially fatal consequences from skipping animal studies. "If there is immune enhancement in animals, that's a show-stopper".

Dr. Suhab Siddiqi, Moderna's Ex-Director of Chemistry, told CNN, "I would not let the [vaccine] be injected in my body. I would demand: Where is the toxicity data?"

Former NIH Scientist Dr. Judy Mikovits says its criminal to test mRNA vaccines on humans. "MRNA can cause cancers and other dire harms that don't surface for years."

-Robert F. Kennedy Jr, 5/2/20 on Instagram

This whole rushed-vaccine-business is why it is so critical to question this whole Plannedemic and how quickly they miraculously had this wonderfully effective and "safe" mRNA vaccine tech ready to go for not only one but two vaccines from two companies.

And now that it was just announced that 15 million doses of Johnson and Johnson's 'traditional' vaccine are to be destroyed that further pushes the mRNA vaccines on the unsuspecting public.

Both mRNA vaccines were miraculously first to market and going into millions of people daily right now with no long-term studies whatsoever and with ZERO liability for Pfizer and Gates/Moderna no matter WHAT happens because it was rubber-stamped by the corrupt FDA and covered under the Vaccine Act of 1986.

As of Jan 2021, it appears that 40-50% of health care workers and first responders are balking and have no intention of taking an unnecessary vaccine for a largely non-lethal illness that has not gone through the usual testing, and has not been tested for long-term side effects at all.

It was also just announced that there is resistance to vaccination from some of those 65 and over so again watch out for a new 'variant' to be released that will be 'more dangerous' as opposed to the latest 'more contagious' to stampede people into the mRNA vaccines.

If the mRNA vaccine technology is really that safe and effective, they would have been using this technology a long time ago. Why haven't they been using it all along?

Suddenly this is the technology to save us and Bill Gates just happened to have it all ready to go with his pet project Moderna???? The same Bill Gates who wants to lower the global population with vaccines… his own words!

The reason they are able to ram this technology down our throats is that they have emergency authorization to be able to skip the long-term clinical trials. This is a ticking time bomb in the arms of millions of American and billions of humans around the world.

In order to get a rushed vaccine out under emergency authorization there has to be no other known and **approved** treatments for the disease (as a result of clinical trials) which is why they stonewalled hydroxychloroquine and other drugs which work wonders against covid19.

There is a ton of propaganda right now trying to convince you that you need to take the mRNA vaccine from either Pfizer or Moderna and that it is highly effective and safe.

These aren't in the form of commercials, because Big Pharma can't legally advertise a product that only has emergency authorization. So how Big Pharma gets around this, and this is actually more nefarious, is they instead bankroll your local radio, teevee and health departments with money for governmental 'public service announcements' which are nothing but commercials for the mRNA vaccines.

Bottom line with this vaccine-business, if it lists 'death' or autoimmune disease as a potential side effect or anything else for a disease with a greater than 99% survival rate you better believe it's going to be my right to refuse it.

A large part of the reason for all the ridiculous shutdowns and quarantines is to make people sick of it all and yearn for life to get back to normal, and if that means taking a vaccine a lot of people will take it purely for this reason!! I know these people personally!

And if it comes to it, I think I'd rather have a bullet than a vaccine which is why all the false flags are going on to cause people to panic and beg Congress to pass anti-gun/anti-American "domestic terrorist" legislation.

Patriot Act II is coming...for us.

The BLM/Antifa riots played perfectly into the 2020 Q-psyop which culminating in the 'insurrection' as the media is painting it.

Patriotic Americans egged on by Trump saw that BLM and Antifa could riot with no consequences and were emboldened by that to storm the Capitol...which played right into the script that Q was created for: to vilify the real truth movement against the New World Order/Great Plan.

The hypocrisy of the left over the Capital occupation is off the chart too.

Extreme leftists occupied the Supreme Court over the Kavanaugh hearings!

Armed Black Panthers occupied the Capital in 1968 and no one was shot!!!

Those are just two glaring examples but there are tons more to point out since they are throwing stones.

And now with this new cancel culture ridiculousness, the media convicts you and the corporations punish you by banning you or pulling adverting to bring pressure from below, and if needed as a last resort the feds will come for you as a domestic terrorist.

Tim Allen. Roseanne Barr. Donald Trump. Mike Lindell. And more. All cancel-cultured.

They are now actively trying to cancel culture our guns...

"Hell, yes, we're going to take your AR-15, your AK-47."
-Former Texas Congressman Beto O'Rourke, who sought the Democrat Party's nomination for president in 2020 in reply to a moderator's question about his "mandatory gun buyback plan" during a primary debate

"All political power comes from the barrel of a gun. The communist party must command all the guns, that way, no guns can ever be used to command the party."
-Mao Tse Tung, Communist Party Chairman who oversaw the murder of 30 MILLION Chinese during China's "Great Leap Forward" following World War II

"I don't believe people should be able to own guns."
-President Barack Obama, during conversation with economist and author John Lott Jr. at the University of Chicago Law School in the 1990s

"If I could have gotten...an outright ban – 'Mr. and Mrs. America turn in your guns' – I would have!"
-Senator Diane Feinstein, author of the 1994 Assault Weapons Ban

"We know that other countries, in response to one mass shooting, have been able to craft laws that almost eliminate mass shootings. Friends of ours, allies of ours — Great Britain, Australia, countries like ours. So we know there are ways to prevent it."
-President Barack Obama

"Banning guns addresses a fundamental right of all Americans to feel safe."
-Sen. Dianne Feinstein

"We cannot let a minority of people—and that's what it is, it is a minority of people—hold a viewpoint that terrorizes the majority of people."
-Hillary Clinton

"When we got organized as a country, [and] wrote a fairly radical Constitution, with a radical Bill of Rights, giving radical amounts of freedom to Americans, it was assumed that Americans who had that freedom would use it responsibly...When personal freedom is being abused, you have to move to limit it."
-President Bill Clinton

"If the personal freedoms guaranteed by the Constitution inhibit the government's ability to govern the people, we should look to limit those guarantees."
-President Bill Clinton

~~There are false flag mass shootings coming within weeks and months to get gun control cooking~~ There are false flag shootings happening now and more coming.

And if it happens and they come for the guns? It won't be the local cops or even military coming to confiscate guns. It will be UN troops and/or drones.

Look up Boston Dynamics on YouTube and you will see that they have already built Terminator drones virtually the same as from the first Terminator movie!! Capable of shooting you dead if you don't hand over your guns and unless you've got a .50 caliber you don't have a chance against a drone.

Since releasing the 4th update last November, the feds have significantly ramped up rhetoric against the 'alt right' or 'far right' or whatever they are calling us truth seekers and tellers.

We are not right nor left. We are awakened to the real truth that they have been hiding for millennia. We are AWAKE and WOKE humanity and come from all shades of the spectrum: black, white, brown, male, female, gay, straight....we are ALL scheduled for culling by the Satanic elite. If you are not with 'them' then you are against 'them' by default because they are against YOU living on 'their' planet!!

And it literally is... this is Satan's world and his people run it.

You know, Antifa sort of has it right, our government is technically fascist and no longer a Republic as the Constitution calls for.

Fascism is when the government takes over the corporations. When the corporations take over and control the government, aka the Federal Reserve and the rest of the globalist companies like Amazon, Facebook, Twitter, Walmart, etc., the effect is the same: the melding of corporate and government agendas to benefit the Satanic cabal.

Remember the quote from Jefferson about corporations springing up around a central bank and bankrupting a nation? We're right there, right this second!!!!

"The central bank is an institution of the most deadly hostility existing against the Principles and form of our Constitution. I am an Enemy to all banks discounting bills or notes for anything but Coin. If the American People allow private banks to control the issuance of their currency, first by inflation and then by deflation, the banks and corporations that will grow up around them will deprive the People of all their Property until their Children will wake up homeless on the continent their Fathers conquered."
-Thomas Jefferson

Where Antifa goes wrong is that it only targets the right, where they should be targeting the puppetmasters at the top. This is why George Soros funds Antifa and therefore controls its direction, message and targets.

We were founded as a Republic where the rights of the individual are protected.

What we're in now is a corporate/oligarchical democracy where the paid-for mob rules, and the mob is used to intimidate those they are looking to influence and silence.

The mob consists of the mainstream media, social media titans like Facebook and Twitter, and also physically with BLM and Antifa. What do all these have in common? They are backed by the socialist, leftist proponents of the New World Order.

So, we're technically in a fascist state right this second as our entire federal government is owned by the Federal Reserve and its underlings the globalist, multi-national corporations.

So now that they are convincing everyone that the real Truth Movement is a white-supremacist/domestic terror movement, they are going to censor and attempt to cancel us on one end, and spy on/harass us on the other.

Remember how Obama turned the IRS loose on conservatives when he was President? That's a FACT.

Hopefully I don't need to tell you that your phone is listening 24/7 to your words, as is the camera on BOTH sides of the phone recording everything they take in, snooping through your house with AI looking for what products you buy and even how big your house is and what all you have in it!

Everything digital they can gather goes into your NSA file in Utah... FACT. Every telephone conversation. Text. Email. Images. Browsing history. Everything from your phone's cameras and microphone. Location tracking history of your phone. Etc. Etc. Etc.

I put tape over my phone's cameras and rarely use them. Someone needs to invent a phone case that has a slide-over-camera panel on both sides...! And some sort of damper for the mic while they're at it.

REAL ID is coming as of October 2021, you will have to carry an RFID chip on you at all times if you are accessing a federal government building, flying or using a passport. Smart drivers' licenses outfitted with RFID chips also via the states to locally track you. All debit/credit cards already have an RFID chip in them to track your every move. They're tightening the noose. We're only a couple steps away from mandatory RFID chipping for the citizens. We're sliding fast towards the Mark of the Beast and I'm not surprised one bit.

Well, Amazon cut off my first book's advertising last October 2020 saying it was too controversial of a book to put those kinds of 'offensive' ads out into the public realm.

With the bolstering of advertising and the uncertainty of the pandemic in the early days of 2020 my first book started to go viral and it looked like I may have been able to make enough money to hang up my hammer and start writing full time…then Amazon pulled the plug.

Facebook cut off all my advertising about 3 years ago at this point. I'm just running on word of mouth right now on Amazon and I appreciate all my friends out there have done to throw in with me, leave book reviews on Amazon and elsewhere, and generally spread the word of my books. Not a mainstream publisher out there that would dare publish my books, so here we are.

People can talk about what I write about and try to categorize it all they want but all I'm talking about is how Biblical prophecy is occurring today and showing how that is.

I'm not a conspiracy theorist. I'm not alt-right. I'm not an anarchist and I'm sure not a domestic terrorist. I'm just a guy on a quest for the truth. I would love to see how many FBI personnel that have been assigned to me over the years have woken up by reading my first book.

You better believe that people like me who aren't afraid to speak their mind about how things really are and who have a significant impact on the public have been assigned FBI agents because one of them showed up at one of my Facebook friend's house unannounced and he live-streamed the whole thing!

Unfortunately, with the way things are currently headed, I'm expecting to be blacklisted from Amazon and others by the end of this year. In fact, this could very well be the last update from me and then you won't hear from me again until I've got the third book done and I'll publish on my website, which you should write down, samaritansentinel(dot)com.

I'm not selling paperbacks myself but if I need to I will at that website. For now, it's a time-saver just having Amazon deal with it, and I'm short on time on many fronts.

And on THAT note, I hope to talk to you again soon my friend! We'll see...

Yah bless to you and yours and thanks for your support!

-Sentinel Jeff Hays